# The Moon Is Not Enough

# The Moon Is Not Enough

**Mary Irwin**
*with Madalene Harris*

Pickering & Inglis
LONDON · GLASGOW

© 1978 by The Zondervan Corporation
Grand Rapids, Michigan


First Pickering & Inglis Paperback edition 1979

ISBN 0 7208 0446 9
Cat. No. 01/1325


This edition is issued by special arrangement with Zondervan Publishing House the American publishers.

This book is dedicated to the glory of God

*How can I say thanks for the things You have done for me?*
*Things so undeserved, yet You give to prove Your love for me.*
*The voices of a million angels could not express my gratitude;*
*All that I am and ever hope to be, I owe it all to Thee.**

# Contents

> *"Do you,*
> *James Irwin,*
> *take Mary Monroe*
> *to be your wife,*
> *to have and to hold from this day forward,*
> *for better or for worse,*
> *for richer or for poorer,*
> *in sickness and in health,*
> *to love and to cherish,*
> *till death. . . ."*

> *"I do."*

And I did on September 4, 1959, in Seattle, Washington. We were so in love that I did not hesitate to enter into a relationship that was destined for trouble. My first marriage to another Mary had ended in divorce because of immaturity, lack of leadership, and religious differences. Now, at the age of twenty-nine, I was making a lifetime commitment to the young woman who was about to deliver my first child. I had wanted this marriage much earlier, but Mary had rejected me on the advice of her family. As a result of this rejection, I had serious misgivings, but I knew I had a responsibility to the life about to be born. In the pages that follow, you will learn of the problems we encountered as two rebellious people endeavoring to live together.

Many times Mary accused me of being noncommunicative, but I am naturally shy and retiring, a quiet man at home and at work. I usually have little to say. Her disappointment with me as a spiritual leader of our family was fully justified. I knew that I should be leading my family in spiritual matters, but I did a miserable job. I felt somewhat denied because Mary clung to her own church affiliation. People with problems produce problem marriages, so we couldn't help but have that kind of marriage.

Our life together took us from Seattle to Dayton to the Mojave to Colorado Springs to Houston and back to Colorado Springs. I had told Mary we probably would enjoy glamorous overseas assignments. Instead, it was a rough road with many disappointments. There were, however, happy moments too. When all seemed lost, the sunshine often broke through and hope was temporarily restored.

In my book, *To Rule the Night*, I indicated that Mary and I were having marriage problems. Sometimes they appeared so monumental that I wondered if I could properly devote myself to my space mission.

Now as I look back on eighteen years of marriage to Mary, I realize that we have come a long way in resolving our problems. We are continuing to change as we grow, and our problems, though not completely solved, are fewer now, and our marriage has turned out better than anyone predicted back in 1959—including me.

The flight to the moon did place special stress on our family. In the years of preparation, I had to spend much time away from home. The instant fame of the flight placed us in the public eye, and the public did expect a great deal from us. On that flight, my eyes were opened to see the earth in a new way, and I returned with new appreciation of our earth home, the people on it, and especially my family. It was time for a new beginning.

I am now doing all that I can to be the spiritual leader of the Irwin family. Mary and I have given our lives to the Lord and seek His daily direction. We had made all the wrong moves, but the Lord intervened in a dramatic way and turned disappointment into His appointment.

Read on, and you will learn how He did it.

JIM IRWIN

# The Beginning of It All

If ever there were dreams that were lofty and noble
  They were mine at the start;
And the hopes for life's best were the hopes that I harbored
  Down deep in my heart.

"Too bad you were out of the office, Mary," an excited voice greeted me almost before I walked through the door.

"What could have happened during lunch that I'd care about?" I nonchalantly replied.

"Oh, nothing much, I guess. Just that a handsome pilot came in," my boss's wife continued. "Let's see, his name was Jim. Jim Irwin, I believe."

Sauntering across the room towards my desk, I pretended total indifference. To show an interest might indicate I was not the eagerly sought-after prize I had led everybody to believe. While shuffling through a stack of papers to be filed, I half mumbled, "Why did he come here?"

"To tell you the truth," Anne excitedly continued, "I think he wanted to meet you. He found out somehow that we had a new receptionist who models on the side."

"Who in the world told him that?" I answered in a tone of disgust, although secretly delighted.

"You know how word gets around, Mary," Anne shrugged and returned to her work.

At nearly twenty-one, the thought of a handsome pilot was more than intriguing. As the afternoon wore on, I found myself completely absorbed with this Jim Irwin. *What did he look like? Was he short? Tall? Dark? Blond? Jim Irwin*, I mused. *That's a good-sounding name.*

Not daring to bring up the subject again after my seeming

indifference, I desperately wanted to ask if this Jim Irwin had said he'd be returning. Would I have a chance to meet him? If he really came to meet me, as Anne thought, wouldn't he be back?

Anticipation rose and fell with each person entering the little photography shop where I worked. To accomplish anything constructive for the rest of the day was impossible.

By four o'clock, however, I was sure he wouldn't be back. A dark, depressed mood now settled over me. It was Friday, and what might have been an exciting weekend slipped hopelessly out of sight.

Another tedious hour of work to go. The tiny, cramped reception room became unbearably confining, and I wasn't sure I could survive even another hour. When the door swung open at 4:30, in my effort to appear diligent and constructively busy, I didn't even look up. It was more of an irritation than anything else to have a customer appearing this late in the day.

"You must be Mary," an affable, deeply masculine voice broke the silence.

Startled, I looked up into the most intent, expressive brown eyes I'd ever seen, and though inwardly shaken, I pulled myself together enough to answer calmly, "That's right. And who might you be?"

There really was no question in my mind. I knew this man in the bulky pale yellow sweater and pin-striped slacks was Jim Irwin. I stared at this absolute dream of a man who was smiling down at me. Anne had been right. Handsome pilot indeed.

"I'm Jim Irwin, and this is my brother Chuck."

Having been totally oblivious to the person standing slightly behind him, I was glad to divert my attention from those eyes which never left me. I had begun to feel self-conscious and was finding it hard to appear composed.

Chuck and I chatted gaily about nothing and laughed for several minutes. Purposely I ignored Jim, using a bit of reverse psychology. When I did return my attention to him, my heart must have skipped a beat, and an excitement I'd never known welled up.

Not that I believed in love at first sight. Certainly I didn't. That was only for fairy tales and fantasies. Yet as I gazed into those piercing eyes that seemed to look all the way to my heart, I knew Jim Irwin was special.

The city bus I rode home after work was due in ten minutes. I hated the trip. On normal days the five o'clock rush-hour crowd jammed the bus so I usually had to stand, precariously hanging onto the overhead strap and trying to balance through jerky stops and starts at every block. During this busy pre-Christmas holiday week, however, tired, package-laden shoppers vied with downtown office workers for precious space, and full buses often passed without stopping, making my weary workday even longer. I began to clear my desk, reluctant to leave, but hoping to slip out a few minutes early and gain a slight edge on the five o'clockers.

When Jim realized I was closing up the little shop, he asked hurriedly, "Couldn't we drop you off? My car is outside, and it might save you some time."

Greatly relieved that this fascinating encounter would not end so soon, I answered immediately. "Are you sure it wouldn't be too much trouble?"

All the way home I had a strange and uncomfortable feeling. Many years later Jim confessed that it had been a toss-up between the brothers as to who would get the first date. Jim had won.

As we pulled into the drive, it became obvious that my parents were gone and nobody was home. When I seached for my house key, I realized that in hastily changing purses that morning to match my color scheme for the day, I had inadvertently left the key in the tiny, flat pocket inside the unused purse. "How am I going to get in?" I groaned. Dusk was descending.

"Oh, don't worry," Jim said confidently. "I think I can help— matter of fact, I'll make a deal with you. I'll get you into your house if you'll go out with me tonight."

*Such a deal*, I thought. *Either way, I win.*

Just as Jim was taking the door off its hinges, a familiar car drove up, and all I could see was my mother's angry expression. What a humiliating introduction to my parents this had turned out to be.

"Young man, what's going on here?" my mother demanded. While I was struggling to explain, Jim and Chuck silently slipped away.

Though small in stature, my mother was a stern, forbidding woman, and to say I deeply feared her uncompromising wrath would be no slight exaggeration. To avoid confrontation with this diminutive taskmaster was the simplest solution to my conflicts with parental authority and became my cautious policy.

With a flock of ten children born in rapid succession, my mother meant business. It was a question of survival on her part, although I neither understood nor cared to understand my mother's problems at this point in my life. Only mine were important.

My father was exactly the opposite. Easygoing, lenient, indulgent to the point of pampering, subdued, gentle, he could always be counted on to sympathize with me. If I could get to my father first, I was fairly assured of an easier time with mother. His intervention, when he dared oppose her, was all that could soften her rigid, unbending decisions.

By the time Jim called on the telephone later that evening to determine the advisability of coming for me, things had settled down considerably. In fact, I thought I almost detected a trace of remorse in my mother that she had behaved so badly, although she never would have admitted it.

Uneventful as was the simple evening of dinner together and a movie afterwards, I couldn't remember a more exhilarating occasion than that first date. We might have eaten dog food for all I cared. Jim was comfortable to be with, and I found myself talking easily and feeling as if I had known him forever.

The next day Jim and Chuck and his date picked me up early in the afternoon, and we drove to Santa Cruz to spend the day on the beach. Jim and I walked the beach for hours, deep in conversation. We had much to say to each other, and with Jim stationed at an Air Force base more than halfway across the country, how could we know there would be time to say it all? I remember with what detail I described the long-range, glamorous career firmly fixed in my mind. There was no reason I could not achieve it. My enthusiasm was limitless. Was I not already in the midst of entering the Miss California pageant for which I had purchased the most flattering, exquisite pink gown my modest income would afford?

Just to be with Jim was stimulating; I had never met anyone who impressed me so deeply. In that conversation on the beach, we were able to share our innermost thoughts, hopes, and dreams for the future.

We had time for two more dates before Christmas and the long-planned ski trip to Mt. Shasta that Jim and Chuck were anxious to begin. Although Jim still appeared eager for the trip, I could detect a hint of reluctance. But early on the morning after Christmas they left.

The loneliness I experienced during Jim's absence baffled me. I hardly knew him, yet I found myself thinking about him whenever my mind was not busily occupied at work, and often when it was. Evidently Jim was having a similar problem, for instead of staying the intended number of days, he hitchhiked back New Year's Eve day, leaving Chuck on the slopes.

It was an exuberant, breathless voice that greeted me from the telephone booth on the edge of town the moment he arrived. Could he come by for me as soon as he showered and dressed? *Could he ever!* I could hardly wait. Other plans were promptly laid aside, and the more important matter of selecting the perfect dress for the evening took precedence.

Feeling rather elegantly chic in my basic black trimmed with a fur I had unearthed at the Salvation Army Thrift Shop, I spent that last evening with Jim before he returned to Wright-Patterson Air Force Base at Dayton, Ohio. He thought he could contrive a way to return each weekend by offering to fly various personnel needing a trip to the West Coast.

Although Jim faithfully wrote long and expressive letters, and we had frequent telephone conversations (a friend at the telephone company obligingly made free, but illegal, calls to Jim regularly), I was miserable when Jim was gone. My heart literally ached for him, and nothing in all the world held even the slightest interest for me. The frustrating thing about it all was that I didn't want this to happen; I was well on my way toward the glamorous career every girl dreams about. Now I cared less and less about the coveted career, my family—or anything, for that matter. Except Jim Irwin.

Every moment at work I counted days and hours until the weekend. Life began anew each Friday night as I headed for Moffatt Field near San Jose where my beloved would be waiting. I can still remember the tingling excitement of those nights as I eagerly searched for that face with the eyes that continually haunted me. Once in his arms, I could live again.

It became extremely obvious that my family viewed my growing emotional involvement with increasing alarm. Being next to the youngest of ten children was no easy position. I was loved and adored by all of them, I knew, but instead of two parents, I found myself with many. Some of my brothers and sisters were old enough to be my parents, and because my mother was so busy with such a brood of offspring, I never lacked for somebody to tell me what to do. Even though I was nearly twenty-one years old, my decisions were not my own, and I bitterly resented it.

Besides, Jim was not a member of the strict religious sect to which my family belonged. He was regarded as an outsider, an intruder, an unbeliever. It didn't help matters that he had been married for a brief period of a few months earlier in his life before realizing he had made a devastating mistake.

None of these things troubled me. I was not mature enough to see the developing situation, so tension began building between my family and me. Home was not the refuge it used to be, and I began to look for excuses to be elsewhere.

About the time Jim and I recognized we were hopelessly in love, an utterly disastrous event occurred. Jim had become an instructor pilot and was flying with a student towards San Jose and our keenly anticipated rendezvous. The student became wretchedly ill en route, and after a brief bout with his conscience, Jim landed in Rapid City, South Dakota, deposited the student in a hospital, and continued on to meet me. It was all so beautiful until Jim returned to base. Because of his obvious disregard for the ailing student and the "rules," he was grounded for four weeks. It seemed like four years to me.

I became lonely, depressed, and filled with an indefinable fear. At length it expressed itself in the agonizing questions I was forced to face: *Will I ever see Jim again? After so long a separation, will he still care? Have I lost the only thing that really matters?* Over and over these disturbing uncertainties haunted me, demanding answers I didn't have.

Though I kept myself extraordinarily busy working at the photography shop by day and modeling at night, the time began to drag endlessly as I waited to see Jim again. During this grounding period my twenty-first birthday occurred, and my family went to great lengths to make it the gala occasion a "coming of age" should be. Even so, it was empty, and my obvious lack of appreciation agitated everybody. When the only gift I seemed to notice was the picture of Jim which he had sent for the event, the growing resentment of my family increased.

Coming to my room one day and finding a tear-stained face and swollen eyes intently staring at Jim's photograph, my mother tried to explain the family's irritation at my behavior. "Honey, you don't

14

even seem like our Mary," she began. "You're like some stranger these days. I don't know you any more."

"Oh, mother," I sobbed, "I don't even know myself any more. I don't understand what's happening to me, but I need my family to help me through this. When everybody alienates me and treats me like I've committed some terrible sin, I just want to run away and hide."

Enfolding me in her arms, my mother tried to comfort me. But I would not be comforted. For a short time after this encounter, however, she seemed more understanding. Still, her constant fear that I might marry this outsider, bring shame to the family, and lead a miserably unhappy life were more than she could handle amicably. And so the rift widened.

Finally the long-awaited call came. Jim was airborne again and would be flying into San Jose on, of all days, February 14. Valentine's Day. What could be more appropriate? My joy knew no bounds. At this juncture, I felt I had no one else in all the world but Jim. My family didn't understand me, my friends dropped me, and I had seemed all alone, not even sure Jim would be back.

What a grand celebration we planned, with dinner at the most elegant place Jim knew. Carefully I chose from my closet a flattering pink mohair sweater and a stylish black velvet skirt. I must have spent an hour dressing, arranging and rearranging my hair and make-up. That I should look perfect that night seemed crucial.

My memories of the sequence of events that evening are blurred. Only two incidents remain clearly fixed in my mind. The expensive steak I had ordered arrived looking succulent, but turned out to be incredibly tough. As I attempted to cut it demurely, the peas beside it flew in every direction, some to my lap, some to the floor, some all over the table. I could not conceal my acute embarrassment, and if it had not been for Jim's smooth handling of the episode, it might have ruined the entire evening.

After dinner, we strolled, arms entwined, onto an inviting little adjoining mall of exquisite shops. Jim seemed to know where he was headed, and again I was embarrassed when it turned out to be a jewelry store. Embarrassed, but secretly excited. Straight to the engagement rings he headed. Still a bit unsure of our relationship, however, I used reverse psychology once more and pulled him away to more impersonal items. It worked.

Before Jim's plane left the next day, we eagerly laid plans for the following weekend. A favorite spot of mine had always been Monterey, a fascinating waterfront city. Wanting to spend more time together, we cautiously devised an overnight trip for four—Jim and his brother Chuck, a girl friend of mine and I. Our honest intent, or at least mine, was that Kathy and I would share one room, and Chuck and Jim another.

To persuade my parents to allow this trip was not easy. I begged and pleaded, argued and reasoned, until at long last, towards the end of the week, my constant pleas wore down their resistance. My mother was the strict and firm disciplinarian; if I approached my passive father strategically, he usually succumbed. After twenty-one years of scheming, I had become an expert at dividing my parents on decisive issues. It was not until years later that I soberly realized how much to my disadvantage this skill had worked.

By the time Jim landed at Moffatt, I had already learned that Kathy could not make the trip. Even though I casually mentioned it to him, neither of us suggested not going. Certainly I didn't speak of it to my parents. My rebellious heart could only interpret their seemingly endless restrictions in terms of preventing me from having a good time. How often since then, in dealing with my own children, have I remembered with pain and regret my senseless resentment towards the two who loved me best, however poorly they expressed it.

Jim and I made the weekend trip alone. The drive to Monterey was filled with joyous chatter. Never in my life had I been so happy and carefree. Everything about the day was perfect. Despite the fact that it was February and often cool, damp, and foggy in northern California, today the sun shone brilliantly in a clear, cloudless sky, and its warmth penetrated to the depths of my being. I savored each precious moment of our time together. For so long I had felt empty, alone, unfulfilled, purposeless in life, as if a vital part of me was hopelessly missing. Today I knew a completeness never before experienced. To contemplate life without Jim seemed unthinkable.

When Jim registered us at the motel as husband and wife, a sharp pang of conscience stabbed at me. I struggled for a few moments as scenes and faces flashed into my mind. My parents' faces, the church I grew up in, our minister looking down at me. *But they don't understand,* I argued with myself, and rather than delve any deeper, ruining the beautiful holiday ahead, I quickly dismissed these disturbing images and smilingly accompanied Jim to our room.

*Jim and I were meant for each other*, I persuaded myself. *How could anything be wrong when there is so much love between two people?*

*And what of the future?* I couldn't trouble myself to answer. The only important consideration was now. *Consequences?* I knew the possibilities, but deep within was the typically youthful attitude: *It couldn't happen to me.*

Not a cloud threatened our lovely horizon all weekend. We swam, ate in a variety of fascinating oceanfront restaurants, walked the beach hand in hand, scampering in and out of the foamy, chilling surf, picking up shells, poking at seaweed. It all seemed so right, so meant-to-be, like a puzzle whose pieces finally were fitting together.

We lingered long on the beach that last day before taking Jim to the airport, and I sat in the car for hours after his plane faded out of sight, sifting through a tangle of thoughts. To return home too early would undoubtedly subject me to conversation and questions I didn't care to face. Besides, the emptiness of my tiny room seemed unbearable now, and I dreaded opening that door and walking in. Oh, if only I could go to sleep and not awaken until next Friday.

How long I stayed there I cannot remember. I watched the late afternoon sun slip down in the west and the sky become a blaze of glory. The scattered clouds changed from gold to pink to brilliant red, and finally to gray. Darkness settled in. Still I couldn't move. Sitting there where I had waved my last good-bys, I felt closer to Jim. I knew the spell would be broken when I drove away.

To my great surprise, Friday dawned before I realized the week had passed and brought another glorious weekend with my beloved. Jim brought with him an exquisitely fashioned gold watch to seal our engagement. Since his parents were visiting in another city for several days, we spent much of our time alone in their home. Not enough to cause my family undue alarm, however. Things were miserable enough, and I had begun to wonder if the fractured relationships could ever heal.

After several glorious weekends together, Jim became involved in a series of examinations and test flights which prevented him from making the six-hour flight from Wright-Patterson. He would not be returning for three-and-a-half weeks, and it would be his twenty-eighth birthday before I saw him again.

When I awakened one morning feeling very ill and sure I must be getting the flu, I couldn't help but be relieved that Jim's return would be delayed. To be so sick while he was in town would be difficult, to say nothing of inconvenient.

I stayed home from work a day or two, but the pressure of business and some frantic calls routed me out and into the office before I fully recovered. As the days wore on, however, it became increasingly apparent that I was not recovering anyway. *What could be wrong?*

After two weeks of wretched nausea and lethargy, a disturbing suspicion occurred, but I would have to wait a few agonizing days to be sure. The days passed. More days. Ultimately I was forced to face the consequences I had so flippantly ignored that first weekend in Monterey.

The warning signals had flashed. I saw them. I considered them for a fleeting moment. Then I turned my head and deliberately walked away, acting as if I were in a Hollywood dream world. The only trouble with those dream worlds is that everything is perfect and ends happily. I had forgotten that life isn't and doesn't.

Now I was pregnant—and all my dreams came tumbling down with awful finality.

# Journey Into Confusion

My dreams turned to ashes,
My castles all crumbled,
And my fortune turned to loss.

My carefully guarded secret became a source of deep anxiety, causing sleepless nights and torturous days. The gnawing fear that somebody might guess kept me silent and withdrawn at work and confined to my room at home. There was no way to tell Jim. I dared not put it in a letter or say it on the telephone. It was tightly locked inside, and the consuming worry soon took its toll. I began to appear hollow-eyed, gaunt, and pale.

At last the day for Jim's return arrived, but my mental and physical state were at such a low ebb, I hardly cared how I looked for the occasion. I was glad he would see me at night, hoping the shadows would conceal my distraught appearance.

By the time we had walked to the car and were climbing in, Jim realized something was dreadfully wrong. As he slid into the driver's seat, he put his arm around me and tenderly asked, "Darling, what's the matter?"

Bursting into tears as I told him, I was hardly able to make myself understood. My whole world had collapsed, and I had been living in the blackest despair for many days now.

Expecting him to be as distressed as I was, his reply came as a total surprise. "That's wonderful!" he exclaimed. "Let's get married right away." It was almost as if he had hoped for this turn of events.

The relief I experienced was like a huge weight suddenly lifted from my heart, and I dried my tear-stained face as we happily exchanged ideas for our wedding. We both knew of the tiny chapel at Brookdale Lodge with a sparkling stream flowing through it. It seated around fifty, so it would be perfect for a simple, lovely ceremony with only our families in attendance.

Before taking me to dinner, Jim drove to Brookdale so we could explore again the little chapel we remembered and reserve it for mid-April, just a little more than three weeks away.

How perfect it was. The picturesque, rough cedar building with a small wooden cross, set a short distance from the lodge amidst a pine grove, was almost idyllic. Hand in hand, Jim and I inspected the charming interior and every rustic appointment. A natural rock formation with the little stream gurgling through it formed the altar and part of the front wall of the unique structure.

We solemnly rehearsed our parts. Slowly I walked down the short center aisle to Jim, who was soberly waiting at the front. Our serious faces soon broke into laughter, and we fell into each other's arms as if we had not a care in the world. The grief of past weeks seemed thoroughly washed away.

Except that the difficult part lay just ahead. How difficult, I could not anticipate. We must tell my parents. We both agreed it would be better for me to break the news alone. I knew they would object to our marriage, but I counted on my father to soften, as always he did, and give his permission. After all, I was twenty-one.

I had miscalculated. I had forgotten that one of my brothers was in the midst of divorce proceedings, the direct result of mixed marriage problems.

We had eaten hurriedly so I could be home early enough to catch all the family together. Seated at the table for a late dinner, there they were. I gathered my courage, stood before my father, and related my joyful news, "Jim and I are getting married in three weeks."

Abruptly laying down his fork and almost choking on the food in his mouth, my father stared at me several minutes. I saw his face grow white, then red, as he said angrily, "Sister, I can't believe you would go ahead and marry out of the church when you can see what your brother is going through right now. Are you out of your mind?"

Now I was angry. "Dad," I stated firmly, "it's wrong to bring a child into the world without a father."

Thoroughly stunned, as if he hadn't understood my statement correctly, he blurted, "What?"

"You heard me," came my calm reply.

Throwing his napkin on the table, he immediately rose and stalked away. The others looked at each other uneasily, shifted a bit, then one by one left the table and me standing alone in the dining room. Not knowing what else to do, I went to my room, lay on my bed, and tried to sort out this unexpected turn of circumstances. The prematurely dried tears came back.

Not knowing where to turn, my mother immediately sought out the brother whose marriage had failed. After telling him my distressing situation, my usually calm, unemotional, take-everything-in-stride mother ended up sobbing in my brother's arms.

At length she came home, strode into my room, and asked me to take a walk with her. Confused as I was, I realized it would be impossible for her to discuss anything calmly face to face. She was too accustomed to ordering and demanding without question. Under cover of the late evening darkness, there would be more freedom to try to express what was in her heart.

We walked many blocks down the street from our home, and my mother talked long and earnestly to me. The only thing she said that I remember precisely, word for word, was a statement that would remain and recur for a long, long time. "The shadows are never lifted from a home where there is a mixed marriage," she solemnly repeated. In the years to come, as problems and crises arose one after another, these words came back to me and caused indescribable foreboding and uncertainty.

From that conversation, two things were painfully obvious to me. If I married Jim, my mother was certain it could not last. "Whenever you *have* to get married," she carefully explained, "your husband will always throw this up to you. He will say, 'Well, I *had* to marry you. I couldn't get out of it.'" It was also clear that she blamed Jim entirely for this pregnancy.

The next evening my parents arranged for our pastor to come and counsel with me. The three of them firmly agreed that I should not marry out of the church. Their considered opinion and advice was that I should stay with one of my older sisters, have the baby, place it for adoption, go to college, and try to pick up the scattered pieces of my life and start over again.

One of my brothers began pressing me to have an abortion. Although an illegal procedure at that time, he promised to find a doctor who could safely perform the operation.

My friends at work advised, "Go ahead and marry him. You love him, don't you?"

My father and another brother and sister kept quoting to me, "Be not unequally yoked together."

By the time everybody I knew had given their conflicting opinions, warnings, and advice, I was so utterly confused I didn't know which way to turn. Nobody was speaking to me at home. Dad would turn away silently, and mother just shook her head, sighed, and clicked her tongue as I passed. My father had already made it more than clear that if I married Jim, he would not give me away. My sense of total rejection by my family was almost more than I could bear.

How could I have imagined the solution was as simple as Jim and I had thought it to be? Marriage to Jim? Such a step now seemed frighteningly impossible. Too fearful of making a tragic mistake, I finally decided not to marry him.

Jim was in Los Angeles at a meeting, anxiously counting the days until our wedding and totally oblivious of the nightmare I was walking through. He had announced our forthcoming marriage to everybody, had been congratulated and partied by his buddies, had our Nassau honeymoon arranged, and had never had a fleeting thought that our plans might collapse. So when my telephone call pulled him out of the conference in progress, he was altogether unprepared for my message.

Not daring to go into any detail or give reasons, certain I couldn't go through with it if I did, I resolved to make my message brief. "Jim, I have decided I can't marry you after all," I quickly said before losing my courage.

"Mary," he gasped, "I don't understand. What has happened?"

"I can't talk about it any more, Jim." Tears came, and I swallowed hard to clear the painful lump forming in my throat. "I'm leaving home Monday morning."

Too stunned to continue, Jim said good-by and hung up. A flood of tears engulfed me, and I wept inconsolably for hours. I began to wish I could die. Indeed, my shattered life seemed worthless, and death would have been a welcome relief, I thought.

The next day Jim made a hurried trip to San Jose and spent the night with his parents. Instead of driving over to see me, however, he called on the telephone. "Mary," the plaintive voice began, "I

22

can't believe you meant what you said yesterday." He sounded hollow and broken, and I knew he was grieving.

While my heart was saying, "Jim, please come over and hold me in your arms and tell me everything is going to be all right," I heard myself answer, "Jim, I just can't marry you. I realize now that it would never work."

I knew assuredly that if he came over, I would change my mind. Or if he would just insist and try to persuade me, I would weaken. But he didn't. Crushed as he was, he wanted to give me the freedom to make my own decision without pressure from him.

After hanging up the phone, the tears that were to be my constant companions returned. I wondered if he would ever call again. How could he face everybody at work, returning without the wife he had eagerly set out for?

When Monday arrived, Jim left for Nassau alone, and I flew north to a little town near Seattle, Washington, to stay with one of my sisters. The next few months were agonizingly painful. I cried night and day, prayed constantly, took long walks alone in the wooded hills nearby, and wondered endlessly what the future could possibly hold for me, to say nothing of the tiny child growing within.

Each night after all of my sister's family went to bed, I sat by the fireplace watching the smoldering embers for hours and aching with loneliness for the one I loved with more intensity than ever. When finally I wearily stumbled to bed, I cried myself to sleep, only to awaken to greater emptiness and despair.

At length I wrote Jim a letter. I knew he had no inkling as to my whereabouts, and certainly my family would not have informed him. Having had many weeks to consider every facet of my hopeless dilemma, I saw only one thing with startling clarity. I loved Jim more than anything or anyone else in the world. If I hadn't, this period of waiting would have held no misery, only an annoying interruption of my cherished ambitions. I would have had the baby, given it up to adoptive parents longing for a child, and quietly resumed my life.

In my letter, I poured my heart out to Jim, telling him how much I missed him and how empty my life had been during these months of separation. I wasn't sure he wanted to see me again after all the hurt of my rejection, so I carefully worded my plea: if he ever had a chance to be in the Northwest, I would like to talk to him.

After posting my letter, I watched at the window each day for the mail delivery. Before running to the mailbox, however, I prepared myself for the disillusionment of not finding the hoped-for letter.

As the days wore on and I thought of nothing else, a quiet lesson was being worked within. I began to understand how Jim must have suffered through my heartless handling of our broken relationship. My only thought had been myself, and in my refusal to discuss the matter for fear I might weaken, I had left Jim with no basis for understanding what appeared to be a callous, personal rejection of him.

Something else was happening on the inside of me, too. I couldn't accurately diagnose the problem, but it was real, and the anxiety it produced was becoming rather a constant state. Not until years later would I face and begin to understand the vague and troublesome emotion which was triggered and began building at that time. Its name was guilt.

The years I have suffered and wasted as a result of this single, thoughtless incident which began with such promise of fulfillment are too numerous to recount. The initial guilt produced anxiety, which in turn registered upon my spiritual and emotional nature as shame, rejection, inferiority, fear, failure, and depression.

Although it seemed an eternity, within a week the eagerly awaited letter was deposited in the mailbox. I breathlessly tore it open and hurriedly scanned the lines until my eyes fell upon one sentence. "Mary, in two weeks I will have a few days off and have arranged to fly out for a brief visit." I collapsed into the nearest chair and sobbed out my relief. After a while, however, I realized I had not really read the letter and began again, this time slowly analyzing each statement, reading into the words all the depth of meaning I had missed earlier. Before laying it down, I read it several times, memorizing certain lines and phrases. Even so, I picked it up over and over again to reread, until at length I decided simply to carry it wherever I went to be able to refer to it more easily.

The day of Jim's visit arrived. I hadn't slept much the night before; I found myself wondering what I would say first, thinking through each word of my opening statement and rehearsing it over and over for fear I might forget or lay emphasis on the wrong word. Then I tried to picture how Jim would look, remembering every detail of his beloved face and form. If I dropped off to sleep, I would soon awaken and start the process all over again.

As the first gray light of dawn filtered through my curtains, I bounded out of bed, threw open the window, and listened to the chorus of summer birds filling the air with their song. Why hadn't I heard them before? Suddenly I realized that my own heart was filled with song and was happier and lighter than it had been for months. For many weeks now I had sluggishly remained in bed each morning trying to postpone the day and put out of mind the guilt, remorse, and grief that plagued me. Today I could hope again that my shattered life might be mended and I could know happiness at last.

My sister did not enter into my lighthearted mood and seemed unusually impatient that I was careless and neglectful of household tasks assigned me. All her prodding and pushing were to no avail, for the moment she disappeared, I would sink into the nearest chair, slip back into my reverie, and stare into space.

The most urgent concerns in my mind were what I would wear, how I would arrange my hair, and how I would look to Jim. Since all my clothes were becoming noticeably tight and uncomfortable, I sorted through my dwindling wardrobe over and over, finally selecting my most flattering outfit and resolving, miserable or not, to wear it.

Not a word of my carefully rehearsed opening statement could I remember when at last Jim stood before me. If he had contemplated anything to say, he also had forgotten, and we stood there for several minutes like embarrassed children, groping for a comfortable way to greet each other. Finally I managed, "Jim, I'm glad to see you."

"Thanks, Mary," he cautiously replied. "I'm glad to see you too."

We sat rather uneasily in the living room desperately trying to keep a steady flow of conversation going, when all the while my heart was bursting to say the things that really mattered. *Why didn't he give me just the barest opportunity? Perhaps he was struggling with the same thing. Or was he afraid of opening himself to another devastating rejection?* And always in the back of my mind was my sister's presence somewhere in the house, possibly listening in the kitchen.

"Jim, could we take a walk?" I finally suggested, hoping this would put us more at ease. "There's a beautiful woods out in back with a path through wildflowers and ferns that I think you would enjoy."

Once we were alone and walking and not having to look at each other, words flowed more freely, but still he was guarded. Always before Jim and I seemed able to communicate spontaneously with total abandon. Now I desperately struggled to recapture that light-hearted openness we had once shared. But Jim seemed most fearful lest he become vulnerable again.

The closest we came that day to the heart of the matter was to talk about the baby. Jim suggested I might like to consider adoption. I couldn't believe he was serious. Surely he didn't mean what he was saying. How could he ask me to give up a life so inextricably bound with my own?

Before he left, we established only two specific agreements, but it was a start. Much against my will, Jim finally persuaded me to see a lawyer. I refused and balked and resisted, but it became clear that Jim would not give in. So I did. I was not to realize until later the significance of this concession and the part it played in our reconciliation. The most immediate result was that Jim would return next Saturday to discuss the dreaded appointment. That was the second agreement.

I couldn't remember ever having seen a lawyer, even at a distance. And if I had, I probably would have been speechless. Something about lawyers frightened me out of my wits. Now I was alone in the big city of Seattle searching out a huge office building where a lawyer, of all people, was waiting for me. As I stepped into the elevator, I was trembling inside, my mouth became dry, and I almost retreated. But I knew I couldn't face Jim if I didn't see this through.

After waiting several minutes in the tiny room with a secretary dutifully pounding a typewriter and answering the telephone, I was ushered into a larger office with rather massive leather and wood furniture. Much to my surprise, the tall, genial, smiling man behind the desk didn't frighten me at all. In fact, he greeted me warmly and seemed genuinely happy I had come.

As I look back, I now realize the random selection of this man from the yellow pages was no accident, but part of a precise plan I was to discover years later. He didn't seem at all interested in relating the legal aspects of bearing a child out of wedlock. Instead, he kept asking such persistently personal questions as *Do you love Jim? Do you think he loves you? Well, what is your problem then? Why don't you marry him?* After nearly an hour of such queries and some fatherly encouragement, I left his office somewhat confused.

If I was confused, the persistent lawyer was not. He immediately wrote Jim a stern letter, ending with the question, "What are you looking for? A pair of gossamer wings?"

It must have made an impression on Jim, for his attitude was unmistakably changed by Saturday. And before I could analyze the rapid succession of events, we found ourselves planning again the wedding so abruptly abandoned.

# Till Death Do Us Part

"Young lady, have you thought about this sufficiently?" the antiquated-looking justice of the peace soberly asked me.

"Yes, sir, too long," came my prompt, firm answer.

Narrowing his eyes and looking straight into mine, he persisted, "Do you really want to marry this old man?"

I must have looked like a child to him. Obviously, he had missed the obvious. "Yes, sir, I do," I steadfastly maintained.

Turning his discerning eyes upon Jim and carefully scrutinizing him from head to toe, he finally said, "I shouldn't sign these papers—but I guess I will." And with unmistakable reluctance, he did.

To that old judge, we apparently seemed an unlikely couple. Even though a twinkle finally appeared in his eye, we knew the hesitancy was genuine. But this time we did not waver. We were determined nobody would talk us out of it. Nobody knew, in fact.

The actual event was a far cry from the beautiful little ceremony we first had planned. Even our arrival at the courthouse before the 5:00 P.M. closing for the long Labor Day weekend was a miracle in itself.

My sister had driven me to a friend's apartment about sixty miles from her home, certain I would change my mind and be back within a week. What she didn't know was that Jim and I had decided not to wait even another day.

I hadn't been there long before Jim called to tell me exactly when he would fly into Sand Point Naval Air Station. There was barely time to call a taxi, get out to the base to pick him up, and then drive to the nearest courthouse. Breathlessly we ran up the worn, concrete steps with only forty-five minutes to spare—Jim in his flying suit and neither of us having had time to complete the required forms. No wonder the judge was uncertain.

After hurriedly signing the papers handed to us, Jim rushed to the nearest men's room to change clothes while the justice and I patiently waited, neither venturing further conversation. I stayed as far from him as possible, never looking in his direction.

It might have been a solemn occasion had an old brass spittoon not been by the judge's side. I could hardly keep my composure as he punctuated every few sentences by using the loathsome object loudly. Jim and I dared not look at each other or we would have laughed aloud.

Finally, after some stammering and spitting, he pronounced us husband and wife. We were both deliriously happy, and in our immaturity we were certain our problems were solved.

As Jim kissed me and put me aboard my flight at the busy Seattle-Tacoma Airport, I could only dream of our life together as I headed for Dayton, Ohio, where Jim was still stationed. He left immediately for the Naval Air Station where he had parked his jet and flew high and fast above me so that he could meet my flight when it landed. As I stepped off the plane at Dayton, he kissed me again and welcomed me to my new home.

If Jim's new white sports car awaiting us outside the airport impressed me, the dingy little basement apartment he carried me across the threshold of certainly didn't. But for a few days it didn't seem to matter; we had each other.

After settling in and unpacking my few belongings, it suddenly occurred to me that my parents still knew nothing of my drastic change of life style. Though I knew we must call them that evening, for a few moments the old fear crept back into my heart, and I felt like a cringing, disobedient child. Then I remembered that Jim and I were beginning a new life together, and this old fear could have no part of it. So I dismissed it. Besides, I knew we had done what was right, and my conscience was clear. The wrong was in the past, and somehow we must move beyond it.

Oh, how I have wished a thousand times that simply resolving should accomplish this. I didn't know then that all the old fear and guilt which had been woven into the fiber of my being were, in a strange way, indelibly inscribed in an inner recess, and that I would be contending with them in some form or another continually.

My parents did not know this either, or I am sure they might have handled the situation differently. They, too, were so bound by old fears that they reacted spontaneously without even knowing the source.

So when I called, it is not surprising that they couldn't receive the news joyously. They were shocked and hurt, and though I cannot remember exactly what they said, I still can remember the keenness of my disappointment at their response. Again I needed their support. Instead, I hung up the telephone with a chilled and empty feeling.

Lying beside me on the day bed, Jim, with his sensitive nature, intuitively discerned my distress, though I had said very little. He comforted me with the assurance that soon things would be better, and before we knew it, we were deep into a discussion on a spiritual level we never had ventured into previously. Jim was trying to tell me something, but I couldn't seem to grasp what it was. It was deeper than mere church, or religion, which was all I knew, and though it was obvious he knew what he was trying to convey, he couldn't seem to find the right words to express it.

At length he reached for his wallet, thumbed through the cards and licenses, and drew out a folded, worn piece of paper. Later I learned he had been carrying this with him since he was eleven years old.

"Mary, I want to read something to you that means a lot to me," he said. "Maybe this will help you understand what I'm trying to say." Slowly and carefully unfolding the fragile, faded sheet, he cleared his throat and solemnly began:

> During my military service in India, in those stirring times of mutiny and murder, I had in my regiment a little bugler who was too weak for the delicate life he had to lead; but he was born in the regiment. His father had been killed in action and his mother drooped and died. After his mother died, his life was made miserable by the scoffing sneers and ribald jokes of the men in his regiment.
>
> When little Willie Holt was fourteen years old, the regiment was bivouacking some miles from the camp for rifle practice. I had intended leaving the lad behind, but my sergeant-major begged hard to "take him along." "There is mischief in the air, Colonel," he said, "and rough as they treat the lad, his pluck and his patience tells on 'em. For the boy is a saint, sir. He is indeed."
>
> I had a rough lot of recruits just then. Before we had been

out a fortnight, several acts of insubordination had been brought to my notice, and I had pledged to make an example of the very next offense by having the culprit flogged.

One night the targets were thrown down and otherwise mutilated. On investigation the act was traced to occupants of the very tent where Willie Holt was camped.

In vain I appealed to them to produce the man, and at last I said, "If any one of you who slept in number four tent last night will come forward and take his punishment like a man, the rest will get off free; but if not, there remains no alternative but to punish you all, each in turn to receive ten strokes of the cat."

For the space of a couple minutes, dead silence followed; then from the midst of the prisoners, where his slight form had been completely hidden, Willie Holt came forward. "Colonel," said he, "you have passed your word that if any one of those who slept in number four tent last night comes forward to take his punishment, the rest shall get off free. I am ready, sir. Please, may I take it now?"

For a moment I was speechless, so utterly was I taken by surprise; then, in a fury of anger and disgust, I turned upon the prisoners: "Is there no man among you worthy of the name? Are you all cowards enough to let this lad suffer for your sins? For that he is guiltless—you know as well as I." But sullen and silent they stood, with never a word.

Then I turned to the boy, whose pleading eyes were fixed on me, and never in all my life have I found myself so painfully situated. I knew my word must stand, and the lad knew it, too, as he repeated "I am ready, sir."

Sick at heart, I gave the order, and he was led away for punishment. Bravely he stood with bared back, as one, two, three strokes descended. At the fourth a faint moan escaped his white lips; but ere the fifth fell a hoarse cry burst from the crowd of prisoners who had been forced to witness the scene, and with one bound Jim Sykes, the black sheep of the regiment, seized the cat, and with choking utterance he shouted, "Stop it, Colonel, stop it, and tie me up instead. He never did it. I did." And with convulsed and anguished face he flung his arms around the boy.

Fainting and almost speechless, Willie lifted his eyes to the man's face and smiled—such a smile! "No, Jim," he whispered. "You are safe now. The Colonel's word will stand." Then his head fell forward. He had fainted.

The next day I visited the hospital tent where the boy lay dying. The shock had been too much for his feeble strength. He lay propped up on the pillows; and at his side, half kneeling, half crouching, was Jim Sykes. I saw the drops of sweat standing on his brow as he muttered brokenly, "Why did ye do it, lad? Why did ye do it?"

"Because I wanted to take it for you, Jim," Willie's weak voice answered tenderly. "I thought it might help you to understand why Christ died for you."

"Christ died for me?" the man repeated.

"Yes, He died for you because He loved you. I love you, too Jim, but Christ loves you much more. I only suffered for one sin, but Christ took the punishment for all the sins you have ever committed. The penalty was death, Jim, and Christ died for you."

"Christ wants nothing to do with such as me, lad. I'm one of the bad 'uns; you ought to know."

"But He died to save bad ones," answered Willie. "After you have sinned against Him, He loves you so much that He came all the way from heaven and suffered and died in your place. And now He is calling you. He wants to cleanse you from every stain of sin and make you fit for His presence. He wants you to live with Him in Glory. How can you resist such a love as that? Won't you receive Him now?"

The lad's voice failed him, but he laid his hand gently on the man's bowed head.

After a little while we saw a strange light in his dying eyes, and with a happy cry he flung out his hands as if in welcome. Then gradually the weak arms dropped; the light faded from the shining eyes; and his spirit passed over from earth to heaven.

When he finished, I knew I had heard something profound and exceedingly precious to Jim. I wanted to respond in just the way he hoped I would, but its meaning still eluded me, and all I could manage was, "That's beautiful, Jim, really beautiful." We lay there silently for a long time, Jim desperately longing but unable to express the thing that was almost deeper than life itself, and I vainly trying to penetrate its depths, but only flailing about in the shallows to which I was accustomed.

In a few days it became evident to Jim that I could not be happy in the dingy, damp basement apartment, so we began to search for a little house with a yard that would be more to my liking. With the limited income of a captain, this was not easy. We drove all over Dayton, inspecting a number of places whose descriptions seemed to fit our desires until we saw them.

At the end of one weary day of searching, we were heading towards the last address on our list several miles beyond the city itself. Feeling too worn to continue, with the birth of our first child less than two months away, I begged Jim to turn around and go home. Never a quitter, he couldn't give in, and soon I was glad he had not listened, for as we pulled into the drive, we knew immediately that our search had ended.

A white picket fence surrounded the tiny, cozy-looking house framed with large, beautiful shade trees and ample yard. Gay flowers were still blooming along the walk, and open meadows stretched around and beyond, creating a peaceful setting.

Without even seeing inside we stood at the front gate quietly, trying to absorb the serenity and beauty of the scene before us. Eventually Jim sighed, looked at me with a relieved smile, and said, "Well, this is it, Mary, isn't it?" I couldn't agree quickly enough.

Early the next morning Jim signed the papers, paid the rent, and made all the arrangements for our move. As I gathered and packed our few belongings to be ready as soon as Jim returned from work that evening with a small, rented truck, it never occurred to me how empty even a tiny, two-bedroom house would be with our sparse furnishings. But in those early days when just to have each other was enough, we hardly cared that we lacked almost everything else. Happily, we began gathering up used furniture from garage sales and secondhand stores. A baby crib seemed the most crucial, so that was first on our list.

By the time Thanksgiving arrived, we were well-settled in our little home. We had made a few friends, taught ourselves to play chess during the long evenings when I didn't feel like going anyplace or exerting much energy, and spent an uneventful two months waiting for our baby.

We had enthusiastically looked forward to our first holiday together and had greatly exceeded the bounds of our tight budget in order to have a small turkey and some elaborate accessories for the celebration. Together we prepared the ingredients the evening before, lovingly and carefully set our table as elegantly as we could with our limited serving equipment, and went to bed with an air of expectancy. The only problem was that our expectancy was in the wrong direction.

It seemed I barely fell asleep before I was conscious of a dull, gnawing ache low in my back. I lay very still for a long time trying to slip back into unconsciousness. The day had been exceedingly busy, and I knew I had lifted and strained more than usual, which would account for the distress.

The longer I lay awake, the more severe became the aching. I began to move quietly so as not to disturb Jim, trying to find a position to relax my back. There was no such position. My restlessness increased until at length Jim roused and half-sleepily, half-impatiently asked, "Mary, what in the world is wrong with you. Can't you lie still, for heaven's sake?"

"I don't know what's wrong, Jim," I answered hesitantly, by this time a little worried. "I'm really hurting. Do you think—do you suppose—should we—"

Before I could decide just how to phrase the dawning realization in my mind, Jim bolted out of bed, switched on the light, and rushed over to me like I might be dying.

"Is this it, Mary?" he looked at me with panicked eyes. "Are you in labor? Get up. Let's get to the hospital."

Just at that moment there came the first conclusive evidence that the quickest route to the hospital would be necessary. I literally turned white with pain, clenched my teeth, grimaced, and held so tightly to Jim's arm that it frightened him nearly out of his wits.

If I hadn't been so scared myself, the whole scene would have been hilarious. Normally quiet, methodical, unexcitable, Jim was never out of control, even in an emergency. But this emergency was different, and he could not decide what to do first. He ran from one room to the other. Finally it occurred to him that perhaps he would make more headway if he got dressed, but in his confused state of mind that was not easy either. I would have sworn he had never been in the house before and did not know the location of anything. He opened and closed drawers looking for familiar articles, but not seeing.

Typically the opposite by nature, I am excitable, explosive, more apt to be frustrated with the slightest pressure. This time, however, the roles were reversed, and while Jim tried to collect his wits and ready himself, I quietly dressed, straightened the bed, a bit sadly put away our holiday preparations (*couldn't this baby have waited just one more day?*), located my already packed suitcase, and stood at the door waiting. We probably would have been safer if I had driven the car to the hospital, but Jim would not hear of this.

Twelve of the longest hours I had ever known passed in that hospital before our little girl was born. The long-awaited child which had brought both pleasure and pain, ecstasy and agony, was immediately named Joy by her daddy. At that point, he could have named her John. I was too weak to care. It was important to Jim though and was expressive of the elation in his heart and expectancy of his spirit.

This child of love and despair became the object of Jim's delight. He adored her. Whatever the hour of day or night, if friends appeared, he unhesitatingly went straight to her crib, lovingly picked her up for proud display, and then more often than not helplessly handed her over to me when she screamed in angry retaliation at the sudden intrusion.

Baby Joy amply filled both of our hearts and lives. Jim had found an old secondhand sewing machine, so my days were busily spent caring for Joy and painstakingly sewing her clothes and mine. Of necessity, all Jim's spare time—often late into the night—was consumed with intensive study. The chill, damp, snowy winter, which normally I would have hated and which should have been unendingly long, passed quickly, and spring leaves and buds were bursting before I realized the season had changed.

# Crisis in the Mojave

If driving across the United States in our little nonair-conditioned sports car was unbearable in August, 1960, what must the trip have been for those hardy pioneers a century earlier? I was quickly finding that I wouldn't care to do this often, if at all again, and secretly wishing Jim had chosen Rome, Italy, for our next assignment when he had been given the opportunity. At least we could have flown there.

The truth of the matter was that he had asked my preference. For such a weighty decision, however, I decided I had better think it over and not give an impulsive answer. Jim and I had been married ten months, and although I still couldn't predict his reactions with 100-percent accuracy, after a day of deliberation, I came to the conclusion that I did know him well enough to refrain from an opinion, thus allowing him total freedom to select our next location.

The choice seemed obvious to me. It was between Rome and, of all places, Edwards Air Force Base in the Mojave Desert. *Why would anybody choose the desert?* Jim did. I knew I couldn't say a word in protest. I had already told him in my most convincing manner that I didn't care which of the two he chose.

But the closer we got to the desert, the more I cared. The tiny car was bursting at its seams with Jim, baby Joy, me, our suitcases, and all the paraphernalia necessary to an eight-month-old baby, including a potty chair I thought essential at that point in her tender history. Disposable diapers were not in common use then, so rather than struggle with rinsing out diapers in unpredictable gas station rest rooms, poor Joy sat on the potty chair much of that trip. I thought I was an exemplary mother—training my baby early. In reality, I was only training myself and saving a diaper or two along the way.

To complicate matters, particularly my personal well-being and comfort, I was three months pregnant. As the temperature soared near the one-hundred-degree mark, my energy and spirit dwindled to almost zero. The Ohio summer with its unbearable humidity had elicited frequent complaints from me, but I began to wonder if we weren't leaving a virtual paradise compared to the oven-blast climate we were approaching.

The first two days of travel were miserable, but a strange thing happened as we continued west. The air grew lighter and cooler. I began to breathe more deeply and experience a new vitality which was totally unexplainable. With the little sleep I had managed in those muggy, rather dank motel rooms, I should have been altogether wrung out. Now I was coming alive, taking note of the magnificent mountain ranges covered with pine, spruce, and aspen, and eagerly pointing out a sparkling stream here and there tumbling over rocks and glistening in the brilliant sunshine. The sky itself was deeper blue than I could ever remember.

After pondering the matter for many miles, delightfully observing my change of attitude and spirit, at length I mentioned the mystery to Jim. I could tell I wasn't getting through. I persisted a few moments, only to be silenced by Jim's annoyed response. "Mary can't you see I'm having problems enough trying to drive these doggone mountain roads. I can't believe these curves," he growled. "You'd think they would try to straighten them." My amiable reaction surprised even me.

Our next stop was Manitou Springs at the foot of Pikes Peak about eight miles from Colorado Springs. After finding a motel in this quaint little resort town, we ate a hearty western dinner and emerged from the restaurant just in time to see a glorious sunset over the Garden of the Gods. Both of us were absolutely spellbound as we watched the crimson sun slip behind those magnificent red rock formations famous the world over. Standing there, I clearly remember telling Jim, "This is where I want to live someday."

After a few moments, as though struggling to focus a forgotten experience, Jim spoke. "You know," he slowly reflected, "this is the first time I'd thought of it—so much has happened since then. But when my mother and I took the train from Salt Lake to Annapolis my first year, we spent a night in Colorado Springs. It was the most beautiful town I'd ever seen, and I remember promising myself that if I ever had the opportunity, I would live in Colorado Springs." Quietly I slipped my hand into his. He squeezed it and smilingly said, "Maybe someday."

Only gray darkness and Joy's impatient fretting drove us into our motel room. We spent a restful night in the cool Rocky Mountain atmosphere, leaving early next morning for Salt Lake City where Jim had lived during his high school years.

Jim had told me much about Salt Lake, his high school, Makoff's where he had worked, the Woods family who helped him through school, Mr. Makoff who had written a letter to Senator Elbert D. Thomas on his behalf which proved influential in his appointment to Annapolis, and the many places dear to his memory. I was excited to retrace with Jim some memorable scenes of his youth.

A day and two nights in Salt Lake City concluded our brief but pleasant stay there and found us on our carefree way toward College Place, Washington, and the scene of my school years. From there we headed to San Jose and anxious parents waiting to meet the grandchild who had caused so much consternation only a few months before.

Mingled excitement and apprehension mounted as we approached the California border. Most of the hurt and bitterness of last year had dissolved into the feverish activity surrounding a baby in the home. Frequent letters had kept the grandparents abreast of the important details of Joy's life—her first smile, sitting alone, pulling up-—all the numerous facets of normal development which took on undue significance to inexperienced parents.

But the letters never touched the sensitive nerve leading to deep wounds inflicted during those long months of indecision. Foolishly I supposed that since I had pushed those miserable memories out of my mind, they were healed. Only years later would I learn that healing doesn't take place by ignoring and forgetting painful episodes. There comes a time of reckoning, a dredging up of all the "garbage" so carefully pushed down into forgetfulness, of experiencing the hurt all over again.

Much too young and immature to deal deeply on any inner level, I fervently hoped and prayed nobody would delve further than eight months ago when Joy was born. For a certainty, I knew I wouldn't. If we could just stay on the surface and bide our time,

I was sure past failures would be swallowed by future successes. What bliss is ignorance! I only anticipated successes, never anything less.

So by my standards, the time spent with our families was an overwhelming success. We talked only of happy things, laughed, enjoyed the baby, visited those we loved best, and spent a few lovely days at the beach. Soon it was over, and we set our course toward the relentless desert sun.

The Mojave in August cannot be described. Neither can it be endured, without air-conditioning at least. In my now almost-four-months-pregnant state, I wasn't sure we'd even make it to Edwards. The closer we got, the hotter it got.

The temperature was 115 degrees, and I lay faint and limp across the confining front seat of the car trying not to complain. Finally, utterly exasperated and hardly able to breathe, I angrily demanded of Jim, "Why in the world would you ever want to come to this horrible place?"

I can't remember Jim's answer if there was one. Truthfully, it would not have mattered. All I could see were barren hills, flat dry lake beds, cactus, tumbleweed, and a few gaunt-looking cactus trees I later learned were Joshua trees. Several people had told me of the subtle beauty of the desert, that it would grow on me, and I would learn to love it. Perhaps five years is not enough, for I never saw that beauty, nor did I ever learn to love it. To this day, I cannot endure excessive heat or barren, treeless landscapes.

As quickly as possible, we got out of the heat and into an air-conditioned office, learned of our housing assignment and its location, turned on the air-conditioning full force, and literally collapsed from exhaustion. At least, I did.

Temporarily we were placed, as were all new personnel arriving at Edwards, in the Desert Villa, a flat-roofed, stucco, motel-type accommodation with cooking facilities. It really didn't matter to me how small, how barren, how confining. All I cared about was escaping the unendurable heat, and I did not venture outside that little room for an entire week until our permanent housing orders were completed and we moved into a rather nice, older home on base— air-conditioned, of course.

My only objection to that house, as I now recall, was the ghastly red asphalt tile floor throughout. Every footprint showed clearly, so it required daily cleaning. The Air Force must have gotten a bargain on this flooring, for all the homes in that area boasted identical red floors.

The events of the next ten months blend into oblivion, and I now remember clearly only one occurrence during that interval. Our second daughter, Jill, was born on February 22, 1961.

At that time, I thought nothing of the peculiar arrangement we made for household help. With Jim's demanding schedule, he never could have cared for Joy while I was in the hospital. Neither was it feasible for us to afford a practical nurse. So Jim's father, Dad Irwin, the only available, non-working relative, boarded a bus as soon as Jim called from the hospital and arrived before Jill was born. At sixty-five years of age, that dear old man took over the household chores, tenderly cared for a busy fifteen-month-old toddler, and looked after me.

"Doting" would aptly describe her grandfather's solicitous care of Joy. I still smile as I recall his detailed instructions about what Joy liked and didn't like, the neighborhood children she shouldn't play with too much, and, funniest of all, his rearrangement of certain familiar objects and where I might find them.

"Baby blues," which I experienced only slightly when Joy was born, set in this time at about three weeks and lasted for months. Had I been older and wiser, I might have analyzed my emotions and realized that the real problem was not baby blues at all.

In truth, a tiny root of anger and resentment was being nourished and cultivated. There are certain laws that if broken can bear bitter consequences. One of them is that the seed we sow determines the crop we reap. Obviously I didn't believe it, because I kept sowing bad seed. The amazing thing was that I never could figure out why my harvest grew increasingly worse.

Jim, of necessity, left hurriedly early each morning, was gone all day, came in for a hastily consumed dinner, rushed to his desk and studied until late. Weekends he took on private flying students. Strapped as I was with two babies and unending tedious chores, I found myself tuned in to a totally different frequency than Jim's—or should I say, tuned out of his. That the communication should wane and static increase was natural. I launched firmly into a pity trip, began to feel like a trapped animal, and watched for every means to justify my dismal spirit.

Curiously enough, guilt set in at the same time. During the few times of honest reflection I allowed myself, I knew Jim was doing what he had to do to succeed. He was no happier than I that his studies were so all-consuming and made a normal existence impossible, whatever normal was. In those moments, I knew clearly that I was being selfish and that my childish attitude exerted unnecessary pressure on Jim. Then I would feel guilty—not so guilty, however, that I changed. For long periods I grew morose, silent, depressed. And Jim was almost too busy to notice.

Jim had barely graduated from test pilot school when our life was suddenly and drastically altered. At the time, we had a houseguest—a Harold Chapman, who appeared to be making only a friendly visit. I couldn't help but notice, however, that he and Jim were frequently engrossed in deep, rather private conversation. Whenever I approached, it seemed they stopped and smiled and waited until something called me away. With two babies, they never had long to wait. Occasionally I would catch a few words here and there, but never enough to really understand why "Chappie," as we came to call him, dropped in on us rather unexpectedly.

Jim had taken on a new flying student named Sam Wyman, and it was his practice to arise at dawn Saturday and Sunday mornings to take Sam up before the wind rose.

Having prepared breakfast for the children, Chappie, and myself that Sunday morning in June, I ran outside just before serving it to set the lawn sprinkler and begin the daily watering before the usual mid-morning winds began. While watching the water merrily shoot out of its revolving sprinkler, an ominous-appearing staff car pulled into our driveway. Ominous in the sense that this was an unheard of circumstance unless there was some emergency. *Sunday morning? And before eight o'clock?* Inwardly I panicked. The two men had exceedingly grim expressions as they swiftly strode toward me.

"Mrs. Irwin?"

"Yes," I nervously replied. "What is it?"

"Your husband has been involved in an accident," one of them said, then quickly added, "We think his leg is broken. You had better come with us."

I gasped, then dashed into the house to ask Chappie to feed and watch the girls. Friendly visit or otherwise, I was deeply grateful for his presence now. Searching for my handbag, one of my sister's amusing comments flashed unbidden into my mind. "A woman's

purse is her security blanket." I understood as never before. Although containing nothing essential for this trip, I could not have left
without it.

Strangely, I only thought of an automobile accident. That was
frightening enough. My first question as we backed out of the
driveway was, "Where is Jim's car?" When the answer came,
"Parked in the airport lot," fear gripped my heart. I had been
disturbed when these men drove up, but the realization that Jim had
been in an air accident left me horror-stricken. I wanted to ask more
questions, but I didn't dare.

I began grieving that I hadn't gotten up to fix Jim's breakfast and
see him off. And now . . . what if . . .? I couldn't face the answer to
that question.

That we were speeding toward the hospital was evident. Baby
Jill had been born in that forbidding structure just three-and-a-half
months ago. I knew the route and the institution well.

There was, of course, no possibility of seeing Jim. Five doctors
were bending over both Jim and Sam, cleaning and sewing up
wounds. Jim was delirious and wild and kept shouting, "Gotta go up,
gotta go up," interspersed with a pathetic plea, "Joy, don't let them
hurt me." He only called Joy's name, never mine, and I fought to
keep back tears of remorse. Perhaps he had noticed more than I
thought.

Later I learned that he was strapped to the operating table at
the chest, waist, and legs with seat-buckle type bindings, but kept
pulling them off. Undoubtedly, he was still trying to escape the
shattered aircraft.

For nearly two hours I sat alone in a somber hallway opposite
the emergency room never knowing if Jim would be wheeled out
alive or dead. The grief flooding my heart was more than just grief. If
Jim should die, I didn't know if I could face the self-accusations
pounding at my tortured brain. Growing resentment of his constant
preoccupation with a promising career had made me sullen and hard
to live with, and I yearned for another chance to make it up to him.

At last a doctor appeared, walking directly to me and announc-
ing briefly, "We must take Jim at once to March Air Force Base in
Riverside. I'm afraid we don't have the proper facilities here to care
for him." With no further explanation, he turned and disappeared
down the hall.

In a matter of minutes, Jim was wheeled out of emergency and into a waiting ambulance. I sprang up and rushed over to catch my first glimpse of him, then instinctively drew back in shocked disbelief. Glassy eyes stared through heavy bandages which extended from head to foot, his face so distorted and swollen with a broken jaw that I never would have recognized him. When I looked at his broken body, I wanted to cry, but for some unexplainable reason, no tears came.

Though unconscious and in a deep coma from the concussion, he was screaming and straining against the straps holding him fast. He lay still only when I spoke to him.

The air evacuation point was fifteen minutes away, and I was grateful that they allowed me to ride in the ambulance with Jim. I dared not touch him, so I leaned over as close as I could with the ambulance speeding through the streets, siren wailing, and spoke quietly to Jim, reassuring him that I would be by him every moment and that he was going to make it. My own heart had no such assurance, but for his sake I knew I must maintain a positive, confident tone. If he heard, I never knew. I could only observe that he relaxed as I spoke, and that was enough to encourage me to continue.

As we drove onto the airfield, a waiting plane taxied over, the ambulance stopped, and four somber-faced orderlies carefully lifted the stretcher and carried Jim out. Just before they took him, I drew close and whispered, "I'll see you soon, darling." I watched through the window until the plane disappeared. Then the pent-up tears began to flow, and I wept convulsively as the ambulance drove me home. The question that kept pounding at my already throbbing brain was, *What should I do next? Oh, God, what should I do next?*

I needed Jim to tell me.

# Keeping the Balance

Jim's parents had to know that their son lay hovering between life and death. I dreaded calling them. Carefully I planned just what to say so they could become gradually aware of his actual condition. I decided to use the tactics of the two staff men.

"Mom," I tried to sound calm and cool, "Jim had a little accident and broke his leg. I thought you might want to meet me at the hospital in Riverside, California."

"Oh, my goodness! What happened to him, Mary?" She wasn't so calm.

"I don't know all the details yet," came my noncommittal reply. "Just thought I'd call you before going to the hospital."

"Well, is he all right?" she demanded.

"Oh, yes," I emphatically declared. "I just thought you'd want to see him."

"Of course we do, dear. We'll leave immediately."

Speedily I arranged for Joy to stay with eager-to-help neighbors, threw some clothes into a large suitcase, bundled little Jill into the car, and headed for March Air Force Base. Since Jill was only three-and-a-half months old and still nursing, there was no way to leave her.

Arriving at the hospital with Jill in my arms, I stood around a few minutes viewing the rather full lobby. Then I selected the kindest-looking, most-matronly woman and hesitatingly asked if she could hold my baby a short time while I went to see my injured husband. She appeared delighted to help.

The stairway was faster than waiting for a poky, self-operated elevator, so I ran up three flights and breathlessly reached room 326 to find Jim's parents already there, his mother weeping over the still, but breathing, form of her son. We quickly embraced each other as I explained my reasons for giving them so few details. They understood, of course, and after ten minutes I left them with Jim and rushed down to retrieve my baby and find a place to stay for the night.

Early the next morning, not even taking time for breakfast, I began searching for a place to live close to the hospital, and I located a small trailer in a rather barren court just two miles away. Since Jim's parents had agreed to remain until I could get settled, I returned home to make preparations for an extended stay. "At least six months," was the doctor's guess as to how long Jim would be confined in the hospital, so that left me with little choice but to move.

Driving back to Edwards with little Jill sound asleep on the front seat beside me, my mind began sifting through the hectic events of the past forty-eight hours. How swiftly the whole course of four lives can be changed. I couldn't believe all this was happening to me—it seemed I must be dreaming or watching a tragic drama unfold in which the players had no relationship to me. A cold chill swept over me as I fully realized for the first time how close I had come to being a widow. And at twenty-three. My eyes began to fill with tears at the thought of the unknown stretching out ahead of me. *Would Jim ever be able to fly again? Or work? Or think? Or be a husband to me? What did my future hold?* My heart cried out in agony, *"Why, God? Why is this happening to me? What have I ever done to deserve this?"* I couldn't think of anyone to blame for this whole wretched scene but God. All my early strict religious training rose up against such blasphemous inclinations, but there was no one else responsible, I reasoned.

At this point in my infantile thinking, blame had to be firmly affixed. So God became the target. Certainly I could no longer vent my mounting animosity on a helpless man struggling simply to live. Anger and hostility were firmly embedded in the depths of my being and were, in fact, a way of life for me. So they had to be transferred from Jim to someone. Who else was there but God?

Two days later in my temporary trailer home, I arranged the few items hurriedly selected and scouted about to find a baby-sitter. A bit of searching turned up a pleasant, rather plumpish woman who seemed to love children. I had never left the girls before, so I felt torn by loyalties, but I knew my choice had to be the hospital for now.

So painful for Jim were the next two months that I was glad his concussion-gripped mind could not retain the details. From ten o'clock each morning until after dinner in the evenings I remained at his side, bathing him, brushing and washing his hair, clipping his fingernails, brushing his teeth, and rubbing his back. The back rub took a bit of doing since he spent an entire month immovable and flat on his back. He was disappointed every day as five o'clock approached and he knew I would be leaving.

It seemed strange to me that I could be so completely exhausted at the end of each day when I had exerted myself so little physically. As I climbed into the car, I felt drained of every ounce of strength. There were times when I wondered if I could even make it back to the small gray trailer and my excited little girls inside waiting for their mommy to play with them. The sight of my bright-eyed angels always stimulated me enough to spend an hour or two reading and playing and loving them before bedtime, but I usually was more ready for that magic hour than they. When at last I dropped my weary body and soul into the bed, sleep came instantaneously and morning followed far too soon.

Morning after morning I awakened, never feeling rested, to face the identical routine of each preceding day. Except for one terrifying day.

Jim had been gradually improving. Some days were better, some worse, but his mind was clearing and fragments of strength returning. His shattered right leg was yet without a cast, swollen to at least twice its normal size, but we had been encouraged to believe it was progressing well. Slowly, but well. So I was entirely unprepared for that horrible pronouncement.

Jim's daily bath, if one could call it that, was barely finished as his doctor stepped in to examine him. Always a bit timid in his presence, I usually mumbled a greeting and excused myself as soon as politely possible. Rambling about on third floor and chatting with a nurse or two along the way (we had become good friends by now), I thought the doctor stayed an unusually long time. I didn't want to leave the floor, but I was running out of ways to busy myself while waiting. I stayed within sight of Jim's room and kept casting furtive glances toward it, wondering at the delay. This doctor was exceedingly businesslike and never given to small talk, so I could not imagine what might be taking place.

Finally the tall, white-clad form emerged with a serious, almost worried appearance, and I wanted to rush impulsively to him and demand *What's wrong with my husband?* But his forbidding look frightened me, and I merely stood and watched as he steadily approached me.

Slowly balancing himself on a window ledge, the doctor seemed deeply disturbed and uncertain as to how to begin. It was I who finally broke the awkward silence. "Is something wrong with Jim?" I cautiously queried.

"I'm sure you've noticed the deteriorating condition of his right leg, Mrs. Irwin?"

"Yes, I know it's badly swollen and very painful." I paused a moment, then thoughtfully added, "But the nurses always seem optimistic that it is improving."

"We continually strive to be optimistic, of course," he firmly agreed. "A positive outlook is always best for the patient, and we do everything possible to encourage this frame of mind. But there comes a time when it is necessary to reevaluate and appraise a patient's condition objectively, then make a decision."

"What are you trying to tell me, Dr. Forrest?" I wanted to get straight to the point and face whatever it was.

"Mrs. Irwin, I do not feel it is possible to save Jim's right foot," he answered with a terrifying finality. "It was so badly crushed and mangled that I don't think it can ever mend itself. I'm afraid we have no choice but to amputate."

"Oh, no!" I cried. "Please, please don't. If Jim can't fly, I know he'll die."

Hot tears began coursing down my cheeks. This was almost worse than death, I thought.

"Surely you didn't tell Jim?" I asked half-angrily.

"I tried to prepare him for the possibility, Mrs. Irwin, without being specific," he spoke a bit defensively for the first time. "After all, he must know."

"No, no!" I screamed. "I'll never consent to this."

With that I ran down the hall into the ladies' lounge, fortunately empty, and cried out my distress to the only power I knew to turn to. "Oh, God, please don't let this happen, please don't let this happen," I agonizingly repeated over and over.

And a miracle did come to pass. Slowly, slowly the leg began to improve. With each small advance, the doctor delayed his decision, until at last there was no decision to make. The day that leg could be cast was a victory. I knew Jim could be whole again. Our future began to appear hopeful for the first time since the accident.

As soon as his right leg was safely in a cast, Jim could be up and moving. The long month of absolute immobility must have stored up latent energy, for now he would not stay in the bed, in the room, or even in the hospital. As soon as breakfast was over, we both strained and struggled to move him into a wheelchair. This was no simple chore with both his legs in casts. Once accomplished, we headed outside into the sunshine and stayed as long as possible. Jim never wanted to go in.

One particular morning as I entered the small, sterile, white room, Jim excitedly called out, "Mary, you'll never guess what happened."

"What is it, darling? What happened?" I asked.

"I've had a revelation!" he triumphantly declared. "I dreamed about this accident before it happened. Don't you remember the time I woke up scared to death and wouldn't tell you what I had dreamed?"

How well I remembered. Out of a sound sleep, I had been abruptly woken by Jim screaming and flailing the air. Quickly turning on the light above our bed, I saw that he was trembling, and as I reached over to settle him down, I realized his whole body was moist and clammy, covered with cold sweat. And I could not pry out of him the details of his dream and eventually decided he couldn't remember.

Now he remembered. He had seen in clear detail months before the actual occurrence what had been blotted out of his memory as a result of the severe concussion. No wonder he was excited.

During the long, tedious convalescent period, another significant thing happened. At the time it appeared insignificant, but it had far-reaching impact.

Now that Jim could be out of the hospital, his first desire was to see his little girls. Joy had been the delight of his life and was nearly two now. Jill was not quite six months old, so we prepared ourselves that she would not recognize her daddy and that it would take time to reacquaint the two. Although Jim was eager to see both girls, it was Joy he really looked forward to loving and enjoying.

I began preparing Joy a few days in advance for the excitement of seeing her daddy, and especially for the head bandages and swollen jaw which disfigured Jim's face considerably. To some extent, his broken jaw was still wired together so that not only were his features distorted, but also his speech. How distorted I had really forgotten. Over the weeks I had grown accustomed to seeing him as he was now.

The special day arrived, and I dressed the girls in their frilliest, daintiest dresses for this important reunion. Anticipation in my mind was great, knowing how much Jim was looking forward to seeing his precious girls, especially Joy. I could picture him in my mind, nervously waiting for our arrival, wondering how they looked and if they had grown and changed.

Carrying Jill and holding Joy by the hand, when we caught sight of Jim, I began running. The closer we came, the more Joy balked. When we got to him with his arms outstretched for Joy, she looked at him, screamed, and drew back in fright. No amount of coaxing, wheedling, bribing, or threatening could persuade the frightened child that this was, indeed, her beloved father. She would have absolutely nothing to do with him.

After many vain attempts to draw her to him, clearly provoked, Jim turned to the baby contentedly lying on the grass, took her in his arms, and poured upon her the love and adoration he longed to give Joy. Joy was crying, I was trying to pacify her and smooth over the rejection felt by both father and daughter, feeling absolutely wretched and helpless, while Jim was enjoying for the first time the baby he could hardly remember. When we were ready to leave, Joy still would not go near her daddy. She whimpered and stayed a safe distance until I gathered up her baby sister and headed for the parking lot.

Jim should have been more mature, and I probably should have anticipated and planned for Joy's reaction, but it all happened so fast that neither of us knew how to handle the situation. The sad thing is that the rift begun on that hospital lawn lasted for years and finally burst open when Joy was a teen-ager.

Often we think we deal with problems at the time of their occurrence only to find we have merely postponed facing them. How much more difficult, if not almost impossible, it is then to untangle the emotional web which has become deeply entwined in our subconscious.

Three months after Jim's accident, and in only half the time originally predicted by the doctors, he was released and we were able to return to our desert home at Edwards. Since Jim was still in two leg casts, I expected him to lounge around the house for several weeks. How wrong I was.

Before the accident, he had received a special assignment. The purpose of Harold Chapman's visit at the time of Jim's accident, I learned later, had been to discuss this secret assignment. I had mistakenly supposed it had been reassigned to someone else, and Jim remained mysteriously silent if I even approached the subject. So how was I to know what was tucked away in that busy brain merely awaiting the freedom to execute it?

Once home, Jim called a taxi and prepared to check in at his office. Vainly I protested and helplessly watched as he hobbled out with a cane. I could not understand the urgency gripping him, and he could not tell me. If he had just explained that a secret project had been assigned to him, I believe we could have been spared the tension and turmoil of the following years. Undoubtedly, he felt he could say nothing, for that is exactly the amount of detail I received for the next three years as to his whereabouts, involvements, and responsibilities—nothing.

During the months of Jim's convalescence, we had grown very close—or, at least, I thought we had. Again we could share our innermost thoughts and dreams. We talked, we read, we planned, we dreamed. It was all so beautiful and unhurried and spontaneous. Of course I expected the spell to last forever and reverse my before-accident outlook. How stunned I was as I stood alone on the front porch, and for the first time in three months, I began another resentment trip.

From that moment, Jim was caught up in a whirl of activity again, stopping only briefly for such occasions as our second wedding anniversary and a short trip to Monterey to celebrate.

January 4, 1963, our first son, Jimmy, made his grand entry into the world. His birth was a thrilling event, to say the least. A son at last! But the thrill was quickly engulfed by a sea of diapers, runny noses, teething, fretful babies, fighting children, and endless rounds of monotonous routine. Jim was proud of his only son, but he had no time for home and children now. All his hours were thoroughly occupied with his work, whatever that was.

I began to realize after several vain attempts that Jim could not be reached anywhere at Edwards. Neither could I wheedle a sensible explanation from anybody there. The more I questioned Jim and tried to pin him down, the more frustrated I became. He seemed always to have a pat alibi, and though I keenly suspected duplicity, I never could put my finger squarely on it. It became futile to interrogate him and only led to more bewilderment on my part.

As the months passed, I regarded Jim with mounting suspicion until at length I stopped asking questions and tried not to dwell even momentarily on my fears. If I just kept frantically busy, which was not at all difficult, I had less time to consider our elusively deteriorating relationship. The perplexing thing was that Jim was nearly always home for dinner; although he was utterly engrossed in reading and studying, he was there. It didn't make sense. If he wasn't running around at night, why couldn't he level with me as to exactly where he spent his days?

Anxiety began mounting, and quite understandably, I became touchy, irritable, distant, sometimes withdrawn. Here was a situation I couldn't control, and it was gnawing on me constantly. It is not surprising, therefore, that the breaking point came suddenly.

If Jim could not be home for dinner, or found he would be late, he would always call and let me know. So it was that he called one night simply to say he would be late. The day had been unusually fatiguing, the children impossible, and I was on edge. When I heard loud music and party-type noises in the background, and when Jim evaded every query as to where he was, I knew I had had it!

Blinded by suspicion, mistrust, and doubt, I wrote Jim a long note telling him I couldn't live any longer under these conditions, packed a suitcase, gathered up the children, left the table set with prepared dinner on the stove, and boarded a train for home. I would prove that I meant business this time. I was through with this cat and mouse maneuvering; he could have his games to himself, if that was what he wanted.

If it hadn't been such serious business, the whole affair would have been hilarious. I'm sure I looked angrier than a pouting three-year-old stubbornly demanding her way as I impatiently herded three little children onto the waiting train. Sitting in silence except for occasional reprimands if the children so much as moved, my mind was obsessed with justifying myself and condemning Jim for the disintegration of our marriage. I was utterly unconscious of a single person or happening on that bustling passenger car, and it must have been torture for the children to sit in the silence I demanded. But I had reached the end of my limited resources to cope, and I knew it.

Suddenly jolted out of my absorption after only an hour of traveling, the train clanged and lurched to an obviously unscheduled stop in the middle of nowhere. "What's the matter?" everybody began inquiring of one another. Those beside windows cupped their hands about their eyes and tried vainly to spot a station or some sign of life in the darkness surrounding us. Jill began to cry, which only added to the confusion. Eventually a conductor appeared at the end of the car to announce that some difficulties with the engine had developed but that it wouldn't be long before we would be on our way again.

Four hours of restless, fitful waiting passed. Some tried to sleep, others read or milled about, one foursome played cards, and smoke permeated the air, eventually producing, along with my inner tension, a nauseating headache. The only positive result of the entire miserable incident was that my exhausted children finally dropped off to sleep.

When finally the motors began stirring again, intermittently at first, our anticipation rose. For at least twenty anxious minutes we sat listening and hoping for the slightest movement forward. It was so imperceptible at first that I didn't realize we were moving, and although the pace increased but little, we managed to creep along for another hour, finally arriving in Bakersfield. There we had the option of boarding another train or spending the night.

It was well after midnight by now, and I was too exhausted to continue on. The closest motel was not close enough, but somehow, I'll never know how, I managed to make it with Jimmy in one arm, suitcase in the other, and two tired little girls tugging at my skirt.

After bedding down the children, I lay in darkness for a long time. Though worn in body, spirit, and soul, sleep would not come—only anguished thoughts, more and more thoughts. The longer I lay, the more distraught and desperate I became.

To suddenly appear at my parents' home and admit to them that they had been right all along became increasingly unthinkable. Although the idea of submerging my pride and returning home seemed a near impossibility, the more I thought about Jim and the anguish he must be experiencing, the more I knew this was my only alternative. A long battle with pride ended as I snapped on the light and reached for the telephone.

"Mary, where are you?" the unmistakably distressed, sleepless voice immediately cried. "For heaven's sake, where are you?"

In the wee hours of that wretched morning, Jim's car pulled up to our motel room, we loaded sleeping children into the back, and without a word I climbed in. As soon as we turned onto the highway heading south, I angrily blurted, "I can't live like this any more, Jim, never knowing where you are and what you're doing."

"Honey," Jim painfully answered, "our country would be in great jeopardy if anybody knew." He put his arm around me and drew me close. "You'll just have to trust me, darling. I don't like this part of it any more than you do, but I can't change things. The safety of our nation is infinitely more important than the two of us," he eloquently uttered. "Please trust me."

# The Year That Was

"Now, Mary," Jim teased, although underneath I knew he was serious, "of all days, please don't have that baby on September 30th. It will be the busiest and most important day of my whole life."

To be expecting another child was so routine by this time that it was almost a way of life for me. In exactly five years of marriage, I had spent nearly three of them pregnant.

The secret project was over, and it turned out that Jim had been working on a supersonic interceptor capable of sustaining flight at Mach 3 speeds and at altitudes in excess of 70,000 feet. After all the self-inflicted misery I endured over the secrecy of this affair, when the details came to light, I realized that had I known what was going on, I wouldn't have understood or cared anyway.

It was with no small degree of shame, thinking back over those years, that I admitted to myself I had deliberately fed my suspicions by constantly reading every mystery and espionage story I could lay my hands on. Then I would slyly watch Jim, carefully noting that he often spent his evenings totally engrossed in detailed paperwork, only to burn it before leaving his desk. And that mysterious brown box which he kept tightly locked in one of his desk drawers led my overactive imagination to all lengths of evil surmisings. "Mary," he meticulously instructed me several times, "if anything ever happens to me, immediately open this box and destroy the contents." As if to emphasize the point, he always added, "Promise me you won't forget, promise me." I was thoroughly convinced at one time that he was working with the CIA.

When the veil of secrecy finally was lifted, Jim told me this new aircraft would be the challenger for the existing world's altitude and speed records. As it turned out, the YF-12A did ultimately break those records held by Russia at that time.

The unveiling of this aircraft before press and public was heralded throughout the world and would feature senators, important press people, even the vice-president of the United States. Since the YF-12A was Jim's "baby" and he would be the celebrated test pilot, certainly this was the opportunity of a lifetime to gain worldwide recognition.

Having a reputation already for delivering my babies at inopportune times, I became nervous as September 30 drew near. I fervently hoped, even prayed, that I would last at least one day beyond that significant date. Deep inside, however, a miserable foreboding that I wouldn't make it began building.

My exasperating premonition was exactly on target. At 5:00 A.M. the all-too-familiar crampy pains began, swiftly gathering momentum. Heartsick, I awakened Jim and with profuse apologies reported my unhappy condition. He tried to be understanding, but it was impossible for him to conceal his own bitter disappointment.

Without a word we got up, dressed, and headed for the base hospital. Because Jim was due early at the unveiling site for last-minute briefings, final preparation details, and pre-ceremony interviews with the press, he dropped me off in front of the hospital.

Suitcase in hand, I trudged up those cheerless steps and presented myself at the front desk to have my fourth baby alone. The routine questions on the long registration form had barely begun when the nurse on duty stopped abruptly, observed my deep breathing and anguished expression, and realized there might not be time to finish. I was thankful, for as it turned out, she was right.

An irreversible pattern was developing between Jim and me. We seemed helpless to change the complex arrangement of circumstances continually occurring in our lives as we were thrust into situation after situation such as this one, and the gulf between us widened. Jim totally missed what should have been a beautiful experience for both of us, the birth of our daughter Jan, and I missed the most important day of his life.

As I tearfully pondered our desperate plight after Jan's safe arrival, I wondered how long fate would deal us such losing hands. The secret mission, I knew, had dealt a severe blow to our marriage. Not only had it set our feet on different paths, but we became social misfits in the process. Since Jim was not officially connected with any particular contingency—he was neither a test pilot nor a student, and the smoke screen hiding his true credentials made it appear he was working with civilian contractors—we were, therefore, excluded from every group and the social gatherings scheduled within them.

With four little children under school age, I was not exactly free to develop friendships, and it was no mystery to me that few really wanted the children and me around to add confusion. So at length I found myself without a single adult to share my mounting frustrations and fears—not even my husband.

I was sensing in Jim, too, a growing disillusionment with his work at Edwards. He was supposed to be the only test pilot there, but after the accident several more were added, and he never regained his former status. Having twice applied with high hopes for a NASA appointment and each time barely missing it did not help his deteriorating attitude. Somehow the challenge at Edwards was gone, and he was becoming bitter.

About that time, when neither of us felt we could go on much longer, a stroke of good fortune, like a beam of sunlight in a densely clouded sky, shone upon our troubled horizon. The timing couldn't have been more perfect.

During our five-year assignment at Edwards, Jim had flown numerous times to Colorado Springs to brief the Air Defense Command. He became an indispensable link between that military site so vital to our country's defense system and the urgent information they needed on the latest missiles, fire-control systems, and interceptors. Although Jim was uniquely qualified to be in charge of the YF-12A program, it wasn't until Colonel McDonald, who had the job, was transferred to Japan that it occurred to anybody we should be considering a move ourselves. We later learned it had been a foregone conclusion, as far as everybody there was concerned, that Jim would fill Colonel McDonald's vacancy.

As for me, nothing could have excited me more. Now that we were leaving the miserable, scorching desert, I could freely admit how I had hated every minute of life there. For five years I had tried to make the best of it, putting on a brave front and trying to convince myself and everybody else that it wasn't so bad. Now I could face my emotions honestly. To be moving to the most beautiful spot in the world, as far as I was concerned, only added to my ecstatic frame of mind. When I thought about the verdure and inspiration of those majestic Rocky Mountains, the ideal climate, deep blue skies, and perennial sunshine, the anticipation was almost unbearable.

Most important of all, perhaps now Jim and I could start over again, leaving behind in the burning desert our past enmities. Maybe all those aching memories would be consumed by the merciless sun. Jim would now have a desk job—no flying—eight to five; no secrecy; always in the same place—and accessible. My heart sang with hope and joy and expectancy.

Already Jim and I shared a renewed spirit of togetherness as we prepared for this new chapter in our lives. We laughed again, dreamed again, tenderly poked fun at each other again. Even the children's squabbling did not set us on edge as it had before.

With our brood of young, we could not move unless living accommodations were certain, so Jim went on ahead to find a house. This would be our first opportunity to own a home. The mere thought of it brought tingles of excitement, and though the near month it took Jim to locate one seemed a long time, I did not complain. To find exactly the right house seemed imperative.

When Jim called to say he had just finalized a purchase, I was delighted. Plead as I would, he refused to give the slightest description, firmly declaring that he wanted it to be a surprise. He would be back that evening with a week off to move us to our first real home, and I could hardly wait.

I had a surprise for Jim, too. Everything was ready for the movers, the newly purchased camper was stocked with every anticipated provision plus the necessary clothes for the trip, and the children and I were eager to embark. Only one small, unexpected detail cropped up. The day we were to leave, eight-month-old Jan had some funny-looking red blisters on her face. At first we thought they were insect bites, but when the three we discovered early in the morning began multiplying, I had the good sense to examine her back and chest. What a busy insect! His name was "chicken pox."

We hated to leave with a sick baby who was certain to share her misfortune with the older ones, but we had no choice. Our furniture would be gone, and another family was waiting to move immediately into our base house. So we pulled out on schedule, took the scenic route through Zion National Park as we had planned, and had a lovely trip, arriving in Colorado Springs at the end of May, 1965.

As we approached Colorado, we had been listening to radio reports of heavy rains, flooding, even drownings, and although I felt sorry for the people who had lost property, possessions, and loved ones, I loved every drop of the rain. After my unhappy years in the dry, brittle desert, the sight of rain and the lush greenness it produced fascinated me. As long as we lived in Colorado, I avidly anticipated the storms, standing for long periods looking out a window that faced Cheyenne Mountain and the whole front range of the Rockies and watching the angry, gray clouds rapidly rise and spread over the flawless blue sky and, at length, drop their precious, life-giving burden.

Jim had chosen well. Our new home was located on the west side of the city of Colorado Springs, nestled at the foot of magnificent mountains. Modern in design with Japanese-style accents, the rooms were large and airy, the kitchen was spacious with expansive windows overlooking the children's fenced-in play yard, and the living room featured a lovely indoor garden with lichen-covered rock artistically arranged with tropical plants. A wood-burning fireplace for those wonderful, snowy winter days completed the picture—a dream come true.

One of the bright spots was neighbors, incredible neighbors who loved us all dearly, even our four little children. Or, should I say, especially our four little children? It was a rather settled area with many older people, like Ingaborg and Denny. This dear couple, straight from Sweden, were like grandparents to the children, and if any of them ever were missing, I knew exactly where to look first. Directly behind us and adjoining the children's play yard, their inviting house with door always open and cookie jar available was a natural escape for venturesome fledglings. Inga and Denny loved every minute of it. Jan took her first baby steps in Inga's house. And it was there the children first heard a great deal about travel to the moon, for Denny always insisted that he had already explored outer space, stopping several times at the moon. Torn between gullibility and skepticism, the children listened wide-eyed as Denny colorfully described his trips and the things he'd seen on that mysterious planet. He assured the children he had made arrangements for their daddy's trip. We all laughed about that, for Jim would be passing the age limit in only a few brief months, there were no openings for astronauts, and it was unlikely there would be.

All my hopes and dreams surrounding this new life in Colorado were realized. Jim and I were at peace and enjoying, at last, a normal home life. The children were growing and developing beautifully, I wasn't pregnant, our home was more than any woman could hope for, and my husband was now an integral part of our lives. If I could have chosen my circumstances from a detailed list of all the possibilities, I would not have changed one iota. I should have been the happiest woman this side of the moon, but I wasn't. And for the life of me, I didn't know why. An aching void seemed always just beneath the surface ready either to burst and disintegrate or find fulfillment, I didn't know which.

I began to suspect that the real issue was spiritual, not emotional, physical, or mental, and I really didn't know where to turn except in the ingrained direction of my childhood patterns. So desperate was I, that I did something Jim had strictly forbidden. Secretly I began going to the church I had been raised in. Everything went well until I decided to take the children to Vacation Bible School that first summer in Colorado Springs. I told Jim I would be taking them—I simply didn't tell him where.

I think I have learned *finally* that nothing is ever done in secret. At that time, however, I still thought I could get away with deceiving Jim and never could figure out how he seemed to stumble into those hidden closets. Stumble does not accurately describe this occasion though. He stomped in and sternly forbade me to take the children back.

Although I complied outwardly (I knew better than to cross him this time), I carefully concealed my inward rebellion. *Who does he think he is anyway that he can control what I believe?* I muttered to myself as I went about my work. *He acts like he owns God, or is God.*

Not a hint of my true feelings did I expose. Our little sea was too placid, and I wasn't about to cause any ripples that would rock our boat after the tempests we'd weathered. So to all appearances everything was perfect. Within I was perishing.

In spite of it, this was the happiest we had ever been, and I began to settle into our new life with enthusiastic determination. Only one other incident occurred that seemed to threaten the growing stability of our marriage.

Adjusting to the new locale, particularly climate and altitude, one or more of the children was always sick. During a rather continuous spell of minor ailments, Jim's parents came to visit us. It was natural that Jim would want to take them to many of the spectacular tourist attractions that abound in Colorado. I wanted them to see these things also and to have a good time while visiting us, but a second, conflicting emotion kindled within as I realized Jim would be taking them alone and I would be staying home nursing sick children. Day after day, as they returned recounting glowing adventures I had not experienced, laughing at hilarious incidents I couldn't share, and planning the next day's itinerary that wouldn't include me, my jealousy grew more intense. While they were roaming the countryside having a marvelous time, I simmered with envy, endeavoring to conceal it when they returned.

After many days of this, I came to the end of my endurance. A commander's call cocktail party, one of those protocol events mandatory to attend, was scheduled for that week, and I decided I would have my revenge. The morning of the party, as Jim and his parents were leaving for the day's excursion, Jim called to me, "Mary, I'll be back a little early so we'll have plenty of time to get ready for the party tonight."

"Oh, don't worry, darling," I casually flipped. "I have other plans, and I won't be going tonight." I knew I would get an immediate reaction which I hoped would ruin their day. Jim's work and status with the "brass" were the most important considerations of his life.

Walking back and confronting me face to face, he coolly demanded, "Just exactly what do you mean?"

"Just exactly what I said," I parroted. "I am *not* going tonight."

Immediately Jim saw the whole picture. He had been aware of my resentful attitude for the past several days, but being squarely in the middle between his mother and me, as often he was, he had valiantly attempted to keep the smoldering volcano under control. That it was about to erupt became exceedingly apparent.

Trying to control himself and the situation, especially in front of his parents, he glared at me and very quietly, but with deeply restrained anger, spoke. "You're making a big mistake, let me assure you." With that he turned, forcefully closed the door, and joined his parents.

My only thought all day long was of revenge, full-blown hatred developing now. Looming enormously in my mind, Jim's mother became the "other woman" in Jim's life, and I began recounting and magnifying every instance since our marriage where she had belittled me so that she might remain first in Jim's affections. "If she'd only had a daughter instead of two sons," I angrily reflected, "she might not be so possessive."

60

The plans I had spoken of to Jim turned out to be a movie I had longed to see—"The Sound Of Music." I became so absorbed in the beautiful love story of Maria that I completely forgot the aggravations of the day and returned home ready to forget the whole matter of the cocktail party. Though I may have wanted to forget, Jim had no such intention. Taking his mother to the party instead of his wife had utterly embarrassed him, and he had spent the entire evening inventing excuses for my absence. So he wasn't forgetting the whole matter.

An icy chill pervaded the house when I returned. Jim's parents were in bed, and he merely glared at me without a word. After a few ignored attempts at conversation, my lovely mood evaporated and the pent-up anger returned. So I told Jim exactly what I thought of his mother after we had settled ourselves in bed. Still no response. I turned my back on him intending to go to sleep.

The longer I lay there, the angrier I became, and sleep was out of the question. Headstrong, impulsive, stubborn, rebellious, finally I got up, found the keys to the car, and decided I would really show Jim this time. I would drive the car off an embankment at high speed and let his mother have the whole mess. Knowing myself, if Jim had not intervened, I would have carried out my destructive intentions.

Instead, Jim leaped up, grabbed the keys from my hand, and thrust me back into bed.

If his parents had not been in a nearby bedroom, there is no telling what might have happened. As it turned out, Jim finally decided to talk, and even though the session began with accusations, tears, and anger, from it came cleansing and, seemingly, a better understanding of how each of us felt. By morning everything had returned to normal, and Jim's parents began making plans for their trip home.

By all previous standards, there was no question that the year in Colorado Springs was our best and the highest on our happiness scale. It was here that I began to dabble in oil painting. What more magnificent vistas to encourage me I could not imagine. Our home was set high in the foothills with spectacular views of mountain ranges to the west and city lights at night like sparkling gems to the east. How I loved this home, our neighbors, this city, these mountains. I never wanted to leave.

Exactly ten months after moving to this beloved place, I had a copperware party. It was April 1, 1966. Leftover lemon pudding cake and fruit cocktail delight were still on the kitchen table when Jim came home from work, walked into the kitchen, and matter-of-factly said, "I won't be able to eat any of that dessert. Astronauts have to watch their diet, you know."

"If that's your idea of an April Fool's joke" I answered without even looking up, "I don't think it's very funny."

"It's not a joke," he insisted. There was a twinkle in his eyes and suppressed excitement in his voice. "I think we ought to celebrate."

# Why Am I Afraid?

In one sense it was a heartbroken Mary Irwin who finally arrived in Houston three months after Jim reported for astronaut training. My heart was in Colorado, but my husband was in Houston. The mountains had never been more beautiful than during that summer I had stayed on in Colorado Springs trying to sell our house. Jim flew back each weekend to be with us, and if it hadn't been for the lonely days between, it would have been ideal. As soon as he arrived, we'd head up Cheyenne Canyon, picnic basket filled and children laughing with anticipation of another joyous family holiday.

While the children splashed and waded in the clear mountain stream, Jim and I stretched out on the flat rocks above them (we affectionately dubbed them the "Jim and Mary rocks") sunning and talking over the past week's events. Although we were separated five days of each week, we probably communicated more during the remaining two than if Jim were home all seven. Nevertheless, being alone so much became more and more frustrating.

Try as I would, I could not sell the house. I kept it spotlessly clean, no simple task with four active children, and though many people loved it and expressed interest, nobody bought it.

Try as he would, Jim could not find a place for us to live in Houston. Rentals were scarce, especially the size we needed, and we didn't want to buy another house without selling the one we had. So summer dragged on. Though I dreaded leaving my mountains, the separation became more unbearable than the leaving.

Finally I told Jim, "I can't stand this any longer. Jan cries hysterically whenever you leave, and we're all miserable the entire time you are away from us."

"Honey, I'm doing my best to find a house," Jim patiently

answered. "All I've turned up so far is a three-bedroom apartment, and I know you want a house."

"Well, I don't want a house so badly that we'll live like this the rest of our lives," I emphatically asserted. "Let's move into the apartment and be a family again."

"Fine," Jim shrugged, "but what about this house?"

"Right now I really don't care about this house." I began to get emotional. "If we don't get our family back together soon, there won't be a family. I'm falling apart."

"Let's rent the house, then," Jim quickly decided, "and move next week. We can live in the apartment until we find a good location to build a new home."

So it was with deeply conflicting emotions that we closed the happiest chapter of our lives thus far. As we headed toward Texas, I felt like a hundred-pound weight had been lifted from my drooping shoulders now that Jim was sharing the load again. But as we entered Houston after three days of cramped travel in our camper without air conditioning, and as I saw the murky pall of smog hanging over the city and felt the muggy, suffocating heat, a little part of me withered inside. I tried not to remember the cool mountains, blue skies, sparkling streams, and beautiful home I had just left. *To be together again*, I kept saying over and over, *is really more important than where we are.*

At first, the glamour of being a celebrity was intoxicating. I couldn't believe the succession of parties, press gatherings, and television appearances; the curious public was eager to meet us or just see what we looked like, and people like the mayor, the governor, and the military hierarchy treated us like royalty. I basked in the attention and began to feel as if I were somebody really special.

Perhaps all that attention was a good thing, perhaps not. I'll never know for sure. Our life had been good in Colorado, we had ironed out our major domestic differences, and when we were elevated to a position of overwhelming popularity, I foolishly supposed our troubles were over. So unprepared was I to face the next six-and-a-half years that it's a wonder I even survived.

Almost immediately, without a word from anybody, I became aware that astronaut families are strictly bound by an indefinable public image—patriotic, all-American, courageous, super family-oriented, always doing and saying the right things. Nobody ever told me how to act or what to say, but a set of rules was clearly stamped in my mind, and a subtle sense of responsibility took hold of me when I realized that total strangers were interested in our children, our house, our pets, our interests, our hobbies. Certainly I did not want to risk spoiling this image, however false it was.

The townhouse we moved into was above average, as apartments go. We were the first occupants of this new condominium, and the neighbors were congenial and always ready for socializing. So the wives coffeed, and the children herded from one apartment to another playing, raiding cookie jars and cupboards. It was fun for awhile, but as the year progressed we were less and less satisfied.

Although we were only three blocks from Galveston Bay, which at first excited me, I soon discovered the water was thoroughly polluted with a sickening, cloudy gray-brown appearance. I also discovered that children do not play outside in the Houston summer. The myriad bugs and sweltering heat make it unendurable, a fact our children had difficulty accepting. Every waking moment had been spent outside in Colorado's ideal climate.

We were the only astronaut family living in our particular complex that first year. I often wonder if that wasn't part of the reason I never felt completely accepted in the exclusive fellowship of astronaut families. So little contact was available that I hardly knew them. Almost the only opportunity for encounter that year was the monthly coffee for wives at the Lakewood Yacht Club which I always attended, but it seemed they all migrated to their own special group of friends. I felt left out and lonely, longing for somebody in this group to care about me.

Mercifully, the year was exceedingly busy, and I didn't have time to dwell upon my growing dissatisfaction with this new life, the astronaut program, Houston, our crowded apartment, and Jim's increasing absence. As soon as we were comfortably settled (if six people can ever be comfortable in a three-bedroom apartment with small, confining rooms), Jim drove us one weekend to Bay Colony on Galveston Bay. I could tell he was excited. He kept talking about the area, how lovely it was, the fishing, the crabbing, the sailing, the wonderful atmosphere, the beauty. I became excited myself and painted a mental picture that I thought matched Jim's description. *Don't tell me there's really something beautiful in Houston*, I kept thinking. *I can hardly wait to see it. Is there anything besides this swampy, mosquito-ridden flatness?*

When the car stopped, I was startled. I had been watching for some kind of change even though we did not have far to drive.

"Isn't this beautiful?" Jim smiled and pointed with a sweeping gesture of his hand. "Wouldn't you like to live here on the bay?"

I couldn't believe he was serious. "What's pretty about it?" was my stunned reply. "I can't see any hills or anything, and this has got to be the worst smelling place in the world."

If I had known Jim already had an option to buy a large lot and the rough plans for a two-story beach house with decks overlooking the bay, I might have been more gentle in my disapproval. But it was clear that I could not be happy in this foul-smelling marsh.

At length we located a lot on a quiet, shady cul-de-sac in Nassau Bay, found an architect to draw up our dream plans (which turned out to be almost identical to our beloved Colorado home), and began building. The task of building a house is awesome enough, but somehow ours was fraught with problems from the very beginning.

Probably our first mistake was that we chose a builder other than the one who had built every house in the area. Apparently it was a foregone conclusion that we would use the one the others had, but we were not particularly impressed with his work. It was not until much later that we realized this was the outset of resentment among our neighbors, some of whom were astronauts.

They didn't like the eight-foot fence we designed to enclose a lovely garden overlooking our living and dining room area either. We thought it was beautiful both outside and in, joined together with small crescent-shaped concrete pieces forming a lattice-work effect. Eventually we knew we had gotten off to a bad start, some of which lingered throughout the six years we lived in that lovely home. We often found ourselves on the defensive, an uncomfortable position to be sure.

The worst part of all was that Jim was gone most of the time. So it was I who hassled with stubborn builders determined to do it their way, slopping about in ankle-deep gray Texas gumbo, unnerved by the sultry air, and grieving about my dream house going wrong. When Jim came home weekends, I could tell by his abject apologies to the contractor that I had embarrassed him, and arguments about the house often ensued.

The children were wild with excitement on that November day when at last the house was finished and we moved. They ran endlessly all over the yard and house, climbing trees and acting like little wild animals suddenly released from a confining cage.

Before even unpacking, the first order of business was to settle Joy and Jill, our first and second graders, in their new school. As if our other problems were not enough, Joy was having difficulty in school. We thought it was due to a poor adjustment from our Colorado move and decided that repeating the second grade might solve her problem.

Landscaping of our new, large yard and constant gardening in this semi-tropical climate kept me occupied, to say nothing of keeping up with four small children, sewing for the girls and myself, learning to play tennis, working out at the health club, and my dearest of all interests, painting. I located an art teacher and began a serious attempt at artistic expression. I made a small studio adjoining our bedroom so I could close the door on the world and lose myself in color and canvas—at least until school was out or napping children awakened.

I was not to realize until several years later that 1967 was the beginning of a turning point in the delicate balance of my emotions.

In those initial months of chaotic adjustment my first brush with the reality of the constant danger astronauts face, and the dread certainty that some would be forced to make that supreme sacrifice of their lives, occurred. It was January 27, 1967. I had already arrived at my parents' home in San Jose for the celebration of their fiftieth wedding anniversary. Jim was flying from Long Island, New York, headed in our direction and was due any moment. As I was thinking about him, wondering when the phone would ring and he would tell us of his safe landing, my father walked over to the television to catch the five o'clock news. It was then I heard it.

*A sudden and unexpected fire on launch pad 34 at Cape Canaveral snuffed out the lives of three astronauts in less than twenty-five seconds. Gus Grissom, Ed White, Roger Chaffee—men whose names everybody knew as the prime crew of the first manned Apollo space flight.*

The world was stunned, but I was terror-stricken. If it could happen to these men during a routine testing of spacecraft, it could happen to Jim someday. I hoped he hadn't heard it so he wouldn't be upset while flying.

But he had heard it on a news broadcast over his T-38 radio just before landing. When he came home, I pressed him for details. He knew little more than I did, but immediately called Houston for additional information. *With all the successes our country has experienced, how could this have happened? Would it happen again? What will NASA do now?* My mind reeled with questions and fears. Jim and I talked of nothing else, thought of nothing else, and even though we went ahead with anniversary festivities, our only concern was to get back to Houston. We left early the next morning.

We were comparative newcomers to this select group, but we felt a strange kinship and allegiance. The astronaut community was deeply shaken, and nobody knew what had actually happened to spark the tragedy. It would take a congressional investigation to determine the cause.

The memorial service two days later was a sad affair indeed. The January air was chilling, the sky gray and depressive. All the astronaut families were there, and the sanctuary of the large Seabrook Methodist Church was filled with grieving friends. I recognized only John and Nancy Bull and Jack and Gratia Lousma, but Jim identified the others for me. From where I sat, only two of the wives were visible—Betty Grissom with her two boys and Pat White.

During the service my eyes were fixed upon those two widows. Instead of listening, I sat there numbly, trying to feel what they must be feeling, trying to understand what it would be like to face the rest of life without a husband. *What were they thinking? How were they taking it? Could I give up my husband for this space program? Was it really worth it?* A dreadful awareness swept over me as I found not one shred of willingness to make such a sacrifice. I moved closer to Jim, slipping my arm through his and dabbing my overflowing eyes.

At the end of the service we all heard the jets roar past in farewell tribute, and people wept openly and profusely for the three brave men who would never fly again.

Often I have thought of the statement Betty Grissom made after it was all over. "I'm going to miss the phone calls," she said. "That's mostly what I had of him. The phone calls."[1] Although it had a ring of bitterness, I was beginning to understand. Jim was gone far more than he was home, and already the seeds of resentment were growing again. So I resolved to put away all thoughts related to the tragedy and make the best of our circumstances.

That was a fateful year indeed—1967. It was almost as if the January launch pad incident was an evil omen triggering a succes-

[1]Betty Grissom and Henry Still, *Starfall* (New York: Thomas Y. Crowell Co., 1974), p. 191.

sion of deaths. Until that time, I can remember only one pilot death—an aircraft accident involving a man we hardly knew while still stationed at Edwards. Suddenly, our tight little astronaut community was jarred by one tragedy after another.

Only three months after Grissom, White, and Chaffee were buried, the first Russian cosmonaut, Lladimir M. Komanov, was killed on April 23 during his reentry into earth's atmosphere. To the rest of the world, that news might have been remote with Russia so far away, but to me, with a husband training for such a flight, it was anything but remote. Again I was shaken, but again I thrust it from my mind in order to survive. I have an idea the other wives reacted as I did, but we were thoroughly conditioned to this image thing—patriotic, courageous, always doing and saying the right things.

In June, Edward G. Givens was killed in an automobile accident near Houston, and in October, Clifton C. Williams died in a T-38 crash near Tallahassee, Florida.

Nancy Bull was my closest friend among the astronaut wives. The day the news broke of C.C.'s accident, Nancy called to see if I would go with her to visit Beth Williams. I didn't know Beth well, but I wanted to go.

No one but C.C. had known Beth was expecting their second child, and as she told us, it was obvious she was both hurt and angry. She and C.C. had had so little time to know and love each other. Now all of life stretched out ahead of Beth with two little children to raise alone, one whom her beloved husband would never see.

Again I reeled with shock and fear. Again I endeavored to forget that we, too, were living with death only a spark away.

A subtle change worked its way into my subconscious through all of these disasters. Always before I had refused to face the thought of Jim's life being endangered by his work. A foolish stance, I realize, for the wife of a test pilot turned astronaut. Perhaps the philosophy, "If I put it out of my mind and forget it, maybe it will go away," prompted my ostrich-like attitude. I even called it courage.

By the end of 1967, however, my mislabeled courage emerged for what it really was, and a build-up of wild, terrifying fears surfaced. *I simply cannot stand this any longer,* I thought with mute, choked protest. *I must know what the future holds for Jim and me.*

And so my mind and emotions were ripe for the next years of stumbling around in the shadows. I stepped off into a dark abyss and didn't even realize it.

# Can the Stars Tell Me?

"Only her hairdresser knows" included a great many more secrets than the old TV commercial implied, and I confided regularly in mine. I really didn't have any other objective, uninvolved listener to confide in, and although a hairdresser is, more or less, a captive audience eager to please her patrons, mine seemed unusually interested in me.

My problems were multiplying with the years. Most of them revolved around the fact that though I had a husband, I really didn't. Being gone 70 percent of the time and then being either exhausted or preoccupied on Saturdays and Sundays when he was home, Jim was almost a de facto husband. All the other astronaut wives were in the same predicament, but they seemed to be taking it in stride. Or perhaps I didn't know them well enough to share personal confidences. Or was it that gold-plated image we were encased in and mortally afraid of tarnishing? Whatever it was, I was getting desperate.

So on that particular Friday morning at the Miramonte Beauty Salon, I again rehearsed my problems. Jody seemed more than usually responsive and sensitive, and I enlarged the scope of my grievances.

My children needed their father. They were getting older and their demands more complicated. Like, for instance, fixing bicycles which my limited mechanical training and experience didn't include. Like homework, particularly math, in which Jim had been a genius and I an absolute moron.

Two of the children had developed serious learning problems which merely intensified the pressures. I knew they were bright enough, yet seemingly they could not learn. I exhausted every

70

avenue of remedy, but dead-ended on each. I knew there had to be an answer somewhere, and I couldn't find it.

Underlying everything else was the absentee husband and father issue. *Why couldn't I accept this absenteeism as a necessary part of Jim's chosen profession? Why couldn't I adjust?* Oh, I knew all the pat answers, chief among them my good fortune to have a husband at all. *Millions of women have to face every day of their lives alone with no hope of companionship,* I dutifully repeated. But it didn't help. An elusive force inside me refused to acquiesce, resulting in a constant state of subliminal anger—something like a lighted fuse ready to explode at the slightest provocation. And the explosions were occurring with more regularity.

I attributed my short fuse to many things—too many children, too little time, too much work, too many outside demands, Houston with its trying climate and crowds, the unrealistic astronaut-family image—whatever was handy. In reality I was drowning in a sea of loneliness, self-pity, insecurity, and fears—among them, Jim being killed, losing him to another woman, losing my mind over conflicts, and losing the children.

After listening to my woes that Friday, Jody, my pert, little hairdresser, brightened. "Mary, I know somebody who can help you. She's helped a lot of people, including me."

"Nobody can help me," I despondently answered. "My problems are so complicated it would take a miracle."

"It's worth a try, don't you think?" she cheerfully persisted.

"Well, who is she anyway, some kind of genie?"

"No, she's an astrologer, as a matter of fact."

I must have looked shocked or frightened, because she quickly added, "Oh, but she's really a religious person, Mary. You ought to see all the Bibles she has in her house. And she always prays."

"Oh, I don't know about seeing an astrologer, Jody," I nervously answered. "What does she do, read palms or tea leaves? Besides, Jim would kill me."

"He wouldn't have to know. And if she helps you, everybody in your family would benefit, especially Jim," Jody carefully reasoned.

"I'd have to really think about this, Jody. It kind of scares me."

"I'll tell you what, Mary," she finally offered. "All you have to do is call her and tell her the day, hour, month, and year of your birth. If you change your mind, she doesn't even have to know who you are. Anyway, she can tell you a lot about yourself with just that information. You'll be amazed."

The line was baited, and I was drifting perilously close to the hook. In fact, for some time now I had been reading my horoscope each day in the newspaper and grasping at every magazine article relating to my particular sign. The mere thought of having a positive, foolproof method of knowing my future lured me in an unexplainable way. I left the salon with the astrologer's name, address, and phone number safely tucked in my wallet. As I drove home, excitement mingled with apprehension.

For a week I deliberated. *Should I call this Edna? No, it wouldn't be right. I've heard astrology is dangerous. On the other hand, if I went just once it probably wouldn't hurt, and I could see if she actually is as religious as Jody says. After all, if she is religious, astrology may not be all that bad.*

On and on the rationalizing went. My numerous problems over which I had absolutely no control and which seemed to be increasing daily were driving me to the edge of despair. Here was a single straw to grasp at—not much, but if I could just see into the future, I might be more prepared to cope with the present. It would be better than slipping over the precipice of emotional balance, and sometimes I feared I was frighteningly near the slipping-off place.

In retrospect, I realized that what I needed was spiritual help, but since I couldn't find anything to fill the aching void, I rushed from one pursuit to another, never satisfied.

The following Friday morning just before my weekly hair appointment, I dialed Edna's number. Jody was right. January 31, 1938 at 5:00 A.M. was all she needed to know. Simple as that. If I decided to make an appointment, I could call in a week. It would take several hours to prepare my chart for a reading.

I was hooked, and I knew it. There was no question in my mind now but that I would call. I could hardly wait to make that appointment—and I could hardly wait for the appointed day and hour. Carefully I selected 1:00 P.M. on Thursday—plenty of time before the children came home from school, and a day before Jim would fly in on Friday evening for the weekend.

As I drove to the rural address on that little slip of paper Jody had given me, I had a strange feeling. Like a teen-ager skipping school to meet a forbidden boyfriend. The little house was several miles out of town situated on twenty-five acres of farmland, and the

72

trip to the country would have been enjoyable under normal circumstances, but my nervousness kept me from seeing anything. I was actually trembling, and I couldn't tell if it was excitement or fear. I knew I was heading into perilous seas, but a compulsion I didn't understand pressed me on. *She doesn't know anything about me—doesn't even know who I am. Could she actually tell me something about myself with so little information? Maybe she'll talk in generalities and trick me into saying what she wants to know. I won't say anything, just let her talk. Then I'll know if she's the real thing.*

The private road leading into their acreage was hard to find, and I wandered around for some time trying to spot the telephone relay station landmark noted on my directions. Road signs and markers were nonexistent, so five minutes before my appointment time I became frustrated and out of sheer desperation turned onto an unlikely looking earthen-gravel road. Sure enough, about a mile down I saw the relay station.

I found myself standing on the large front porch of a modest white-framed house that brisk, early March day, waiting for the door to open. A herd of fat sheep grazed in one fenced pasture surrounding a low, roughly hewn, unpainted shed, and a brown horse trotted in another. Other than that, nothing but flat, treeless land lay as far as my eyes could see.

The little woman not more than five feet tall and clad in a bright print caftan appeared just in time. I almost lost my courage, and darted back to my car.

"Won't you come in?" she said warmly. I didn't want to divulge my name, so I merely smiled and nodded. "Just have a seat and I'll be with you in a moment." She disappeared into the kitchen, and I heard her finishing a telephone conversation.

I was glad for time to visually inspect my surroundings. My eyes darted from object to object, carefully evaluating all that I saw, hoping to gain some insight into the life style and person into whose power I might be placing myself. Old-fashioned linoleum and a few faded rugs covered the floors; furniture was inexpensive, well-worn, and looked like it might have come straight from a 1920 catalog; cheap knickknacks abounded, and nondescript pictures of assorted sizes dotted the walls. The only picture I remember distinctly was a large one of Jesus, and I noticed three open Bibles placed conspicuously—one on the kitchen drainboard, another on a table against a wall, and the third on a small table near the sofa where I sat.

*The Moon Is Not Enough* 73

It was the Bibles that put me at ease. They had figured promi-
nently in my religiously oriented childhood home, and since I had
begun to suspect that my need was spiritual, I relaxed a bit. *I may
discover a real tie-in between religion and astrology,* I reflected.
*After all, didn't God create the stars and planets? Surely their
purpose is more than ornamental. This woman just may have my
answers.* I was pliant, receptive, and vulnerable to any counsel this
new adviser might offer.

As Edna walked in smiling and introducing herself, this fiftyish
woman with unnatural appearing red tinted hair and slightly distorted mouth paralyzed from a previous light stroke startled me for a
moment. But her friendly manner and obvious warmth of spirit
completely disarmed me, and I became comfortable in a matter of
minutes.

After the exchange of a few customary pleasantries, Edna
pulled out the birth chart she had carefully computed for me and
explained each aspect in meticulous detail. Apparently, according to
her, the planets and moon lined up at my birth in a specific fashion
that determined my future life. My chart looked something like this
(the actual one was longer and far more detailed):

| | |
|---|---|
| Birth date: | January 31, 1938, 5:00 A.M. |
| Aquarius: | Water + Air = Life |
| Moon: | When the moon is in a direct line with Mars, be careful of your feet. (Dates were included.) |
| Jupiter: | When Jupiter was in trine with Saturn and Uranius, you had a difficult time in your marriage. (More dates.) |
| Saturn: | You care a great deal about small animals and antiques. |
| Uranius: | You can be provoked to an argument even with a police officer if you feel you are right. Be careful of your anger—it is very destructive, chiefly to you. |
| Venus: | Makes you a Water Bearer; you will serve mankind in a useful way. |
| Mars: | Beauty and music have a strange effect upon you. |

A time or two it seemed she was almost in a trance as she
concentrated on a particular detail. Often, when telling me what she
saw, she prefaced her statement with "God has shown me." That
sounded authoritative, and I believed her.

How she was able to cite precise information about particular incidents in my life I couldn't imagine. For instance, she knew the number of children I had, where they were born, their sex, and offered advice as to guidelines in training and mistakes to guard against for each child. She knew the year and month of Jim's aircraft accident. When she began to draw a rough map showing where we lived in Nassau Bay, indicating a corner lot in a cul-de-sac and even circling the areas in the yard where I had planted trees, I leaned over the small table between us hardly breathing, spellbound. At that time I didn't know she was a psychic as well as an astrologer, as were her mother and grandmother before her.

Finally she picked up an ordinary deck of cards and told me I could ask her any three questions I wished to have answered. I was prepared for this as Jody, my hairdresser, had told me to have my questions ready.

First, I wanted to know if my marriage would last. I had read everything I could about the astrological compatibility between Aquarians and Pisceans. Jim and I had so many problems that I had been questioning whether or not we were right for each other. If not, I probably had better find out now and do something about it. Although Edna did not answer this question directly, her implication was affirmative.

Secondly, I asked if I would have another child, preferably a son. I could, she replied, but the child's leg would be crippled. This, I knew, would destroy Jim's ego as he could not bear anything less than perfection.

My final query was direct and brief. "Will my husband go to the moon?" Immediately she realized I was an astronaut's wife and answered with a firm "Yes!"

The session over, I departed weak and shaken to pick up four-year-old Jan whom Nancy Bull was keeping. Although I briefly related to Nancy what had happened at the astrology session, I didn't go into detail because I had too much to sort out in my own mind. It was at Nancy's that I suddenly realized my body was icy cold from the waist down.

During the two weeks before my next appointment, I tried to recall every detail of my conversation with Edna so that I might reconstruct and evaluate its impact and importance in my life. The rightness or wrongness of consulting a medium did not enter my deliberations. Since I lacked within myself the necessary resources to solve my ever-increasing personal problems, I felt justified in turning to whatever source could provide these. A smug attitude began to develop. I was on the inside of the mainstream of life now, and I didn't have to helplessly wait for its shattering events to occur. Knowing the future couldn't do anything but help untangle my muddled affairs. Now I had a golden key, a simple solution, and I intended to give myself unreservedly to this mysterious magic.

Jim was so submerged in NASA and the space program that I decided not to disrupt his profound concentration by informing him of my latest involvement. More and more we were living our separate lives, unable to penetrate or share one another's worlds. Neither of us wanted it that way, but we were dealing with a force of greater magnitude than our personal lives. NASA came first, like it or not. The success of our nation's space program depended upon the absolute dedication of everybody involved.

Jim's coveted promotion to lieutenant colonel, which happened shortly before my first visit to the astrologer, was one of my frustrations. Promotion parties always accompanied military rank advancements, and I desperately wanted to have a party for Jim. Naturally, he was away. I even learned of his achievement by telephone, and there never was an opportunity for celebration. I felt so cheated, so isolated, so insignificant a consideration in Jim's career.

The space program was progressing rapidly and successfully. Although Apollo 11's historic flight with man's first descent to the moon had not taken place, Apollo 12 was already in preparation, and Jim worked feverishly with Dave Scott and Al Worden on the back-up crew. This meant, of course, that if anything happened at the last minute to prevent or disqualify the prime crew, the back-ups must be ready to step into the capsule.

So overwhelming was this responsibility that Jim and I were losing touch with each other. When he was home on Saturdays and Sundays, we rarely even talked about our children's school difficulties and behavior, or discipline problems, or the average domestic situations husband and wife normally share. I tried to protect his meager time with us and kept things light and pleasant. We couldn't talk about Jim's work either, because I didn't understand it. So communication between us dwindled to a trickle.

Although I tried to keep things smooth on the surface, I deeply resented Jim's absence. On the other hand, after having been in charge all week making every decision and family plans on my own, it was difficult to relinquish control, and occasionally I recognized that I was resenting his presence. All of this, I now realize, made Jim feel cut off from me and the children.

My next visit to the astrologist was less traumatic, and the chart for April was not so detailed or involved. Again I was allowed three questions, but this time they related to people other than myself.

I had always wondered about my friend Nikki, of San Jose modeling days, with whom I had lost contact. Nikki and I had shared many of our deepest secrets and had had many good times together, but I knew she was having serious problems. Her husband had walked out leaving her alone with their three children. When Edna told me that Nikki had died from a self-inflicted overdose, I was heartbroken and wept profusely. I recognized, however, that some of the grief I experienced was for myself, and it frightened me to think that my problems might reach those proportions and drive me to the same desperation.

When I finally regained my composure, I looked again at the questions I had carefully prepared before leaving home. My friend Nancy Bull had just been through a traumatic miscarriage of a child she longed for, so I wanted to know if she would have more children. "Yes," Edna said, "first a boy, then a girl." She did, too, even though she laughed at me when I told her what Edna said. Both she and John had decided to have only one more child, and that was that.

My last question again concerned the Bulls. *Would Nancy's husband, John, go to the moon?* John had been battling annoying medical problems and was wrestling with a decision of whether to leave NASA and the space program. "No, John will not go to the moon and will soon leave the program," was Edna's firm answer. She was right. I never told Nancy about my third question.

In a short time Edna and I became fast friends. I needed someone to cling to, so this kindly, motherly figure in whom I could confide all my innermost secrets stepped in and began to possess me mind, soul, and spirit. She was not to blame. I was. I knowingly and willingly opened myself to her friendship and to her persuasive occult influence. I had known in the beginning that I was courting a dangerous game, but I moved right in and played anyway.

The first warning signal that I was headed for trouble came with my complete withdrawal from everybody except Edna. Astrology became an obsession, and Edna was the only person I communicated with. She had all the answers, and I had all the questions. *What a fool I would be not to listen to her*, I thought. So listen I did.

At length, astrology became my religion. It was, at best, a thoroughly self-centered approach to religious belief, but at this juncture of my life I could do no better since I was so thoroughly self-centered. I had reached the end of my own resources and began to feel that even God couldn't be bothered with my problems. My search for a substitute ended in astrology. I felt I had "experienced" astrology, and deep inside I knew it to be true and believed profoundly in the effects of cosmic rhythms and vibrations. All ability to make my own personal decisions now vanished, and I was helplessly dependent upon my horoscope and Edna's interpretations. In even small matters, I became unable to arrive at a logical, practical determination for action without astrological help. This should have been the second warning signal, but I wasn't watching or caring.

The third was Jim. My initial reason for turning to astrology had been to solve our marriage problems. If I had been seeing clearly, I would have recognized that after this occult dependence set in, our relationship became more fractured and damaged than ever before. But I was so securely bound and deceived that I could never have admitted that astrology was not the cure-all I believed it to be.

Jim never really knew how deeply involved I was in this world of darkness. It was easy to conceal it from him since he was seldom home, and when he was it was in body only. I knew he would object, and besides, I knew I was right, or so I justified my deception.

Only twice that I remember did I press him in the direction of astrology. I had Edna compute a birth chart for him and begged him to let her interpret it. He went, but never mentioned the visit and quietly tucked the chart away in his dresser drawer when he came home.

A few months later Edna made a startling prophecy that threw me into a frenzy. Jim was working on a complicated spacecraft simulator at Grumman Aircraft in New York. "There is a malfunctioning wire in Jim's simulator," Edna said quietly, "and if it isn't corrected, a disastrous fire will result."

Although Jim hadn't expressed himself in so many words, I knew he viewed Edna as a colossal hoax. I had resolved never to speak of her again in his presence, so I found myself in a frustrating dilemma. I was afraid to tell him and afraid not to. Afraid not to won, and as soon as he returned from Grumman, Edna's prediction and a torrent of my pent-up fears overflowed and gushed out almost incoherently. Jim waited until I finished. Then he began.

"As long as I live I don't ever want to hear another word from that phony stargazer," he shouted angrily. "I don't care what she says; I don't want to know and don't tell me any more. There are thousands of wires and dozens of panels in that contraption. They'd think I was a blooming idiot if I told them some stupid fortuneteller said there's a single wire fouled up and let's spend the next year sorting through the maze to find it." With that he stomped out, and we had a delightful weekend of total silence.

Apparently my friends, all of whom had withdrawn from me or vice versa, had seen my problems coming on but felt at a loss to help me. Only one attempted to do something constructive. Unknown to me, DiAnne invited Jim to dinner to talk with him about my involvement with Edna. "It's hard to know what another person feels or knows," she wrote me later, "but I got the distinct impression that Jim really didn't know the extent of your involvement with astrology." Afraid of being considered a busybody, she did not pursue it and didn't know what else to do at the time.

"I was so against all of it," she wrote, "that at that point you and I began to drift farther and farther apart. You did so want me to become involved, and instead of riding out the storm with you and helping, I began to shy away. In fact, ever since that time I have felt like I deserted you and just lapsed into the good old world of apathy. Not very gallant, but all too human a malady."

As the weeks and months passed, I had the miserably helpless feeling of being engulfed in quicksand, and I was sinking just a little at a time. I couldn't seem to grasp hold of anything to steady me and reverse the downward pull. On May 5, 1968, I almost went under. My brother Claire, nearest and dearest to me, was tragically and suddenly killed.

# The Storm

When I heard my brother-in-law Ernie's voice, I knew this was not an ordinary call. It came that May evening as the whole family was seated at the dinner table. When the telephone rang, I jumped up to answer feeling a bit irritated that somebody would call at 6:05, a rather accepted time for people to be eating dinner. Ernie, my sister Donna's husband, the one I had stayed with in Washington before Jim and I married, had never called before, so hearing his voice at the other end immediately alarmed me. *Something's wrong,* I knew instinctively.

"What is it, Ernie?" I asked urgently.

"I have bad news for you, sis. Are you sitting down?"

I wasn't, and I didn't. Frozen to the spot, in the few seconds before he continued I tried to brace myself for whatever message he had. *Somebody in the family has died. I know they have. Is it mother, dad? Or one of my brothers?—they all drive like they are racing in the Indy 500. Oh, dear God, how can I face this?*

"Ernie, tell me. What is it?"

"Mary, it's Claire. He's dead. He accidentally fell from a cliff in the Santa Cruz Mountains yesterday, and we found him today. Funeral will be Monday. If you can make it, we'll find room for you."

"Oh, Ernie, no, no—it can't be," I cried. "What happened? For heaven's sake, what happened?"

"Well, Mary, Claire's two buddies who were with him told us that the three of them and Claire's dog, Sunny, took his van to the mountains to look for a ghost town. You know how Claire collects old bottles, and I guess he was hoping to find some. When they parked the van and got out, Claire told his buddies to go in one direction and he and Sunny would go in the other and meet at the old ghost town. Claire never showed up. His buddies waited until sunset, then drove the van back to town. This morning a search party went up to the spot where they had last seen Claire and began to call for Sunny. Right away the dog started yelping and came running to them and led them to Claire's body. It was an eighty-foot cliff, Mary, and we're sure he died instantly."

"I can't believe it. Oh, I just can't believe it," I wailed. "How are mom and dad taking it, Ernie?"

"It's pretty tough on all of us, Mary, especially Vikki. You know, they've hardly been married—not even a year, and she just can't seem to get hold of herself."

When the conversation ended, I hung up the phone in a daze. Too stunned even for tears yet, I walked into the dining room and told Jim all Ernie had said, then went to my bedroom. For the first time in my life I understood what a broken heart was. A deep, swelling pain engulfed my chest area and seemed to shut out my very breath. Now I began to sob—great, heaving, breathless sobs. Not knowing where to turn for comfort, I found my Bible and clasped it to me. I hadn't read it in years, but somehow holding that Book was the only thing I knew to do in this desperate hour.

I kept waiting for Jim to come in. Even though our relationship was shaky and strained, I needed him so badly that I felt sure he would sense it and try to comfort me. He never came.

*Why? Why? Why did this happen?* My mind kept repeating. Claire was only twenty-seven years old, married less than a year, and he had recently committed his life to God and had become a dedicated Christian after years of wandering and rebelling. It didn't seem fair. *Where was God when Claire needed Him?*

The rest of the evening was spent in a flurry of last-minute preparations to arrange for children, pack, straighten the house, and be ready to leave early in the morning. Nancy Bull offered to keep the children, so it was decided that Joy and Jill should stay with her while Jimmy and Jan would go with me to San Jose.

Just before falling into bed in utter exhaustion, I slipped away out of Jim's hearing and called Edna. When I told her what had happened, a long silence followed. Finally she said sadly, "I should have told you—I should have told you. Then you might have been prepared a little."

"Told me what?" I asked.

"Last week I clearly saw a black cloud surrounding you. It frightened me, so I tried to dispel it and convince myself I only thought I saw it. But it wouldn't leave. I knew the cloud meant death, and I thought it was you—so I didn't tell you."

A chill swept over me. Had some mysterious fate arranged this accident so that nothing could prevent it? Though I went to bed, I couldn't sleep and spent the long night fitfully tossing, trying to understand something of the baffling circumstances engulfing me. It was like the scattered pieces of a puzzle, and I couldn't find even two that fit together. The night was miserable, but morning was no better, for now I had to rush to the airport and the grim ordeal awaiting me in San Jose. The black cloud Edna had seen was settling down over my life.

Once there, I learned that my sister Lorraine and her husband had been with the search crew and were the first to see Claire's broken body. Although I was crumbling inside, I felt I had to be strong for Lorraine and the rest of the family, all of whom were so overcome with grief they couldn't eat or sleep. I did not even allow myself the indulgence of crying in their presence. Why I thought I had to be the strong one, I'll never know. Jim flew in from New York for the funeral, and I was able to lean on his strength that day.

After the service while the family gathered around the casket, the thought that kept piercing my heart was *Will I ever see Claire again? Will I meet him in heaven?* I looked at that precious face and I had no answer. But in that moment, I knew there was no spiritual reality in my professed Christian experience. All my life I had only "played church."

As I stood there, something I had heard in a church long ago came to my mind. Something about life being so fragile that it is like a vapor. Of course, I didn't know where the saying came from—the Bible, I supposed. But the truth of it gripped my heart, and I began to realize that my own life was like Claire's. Fragile as a breath. *What would happen to me if I died suddenly and had to face God?* How frightening the thought became.

I returned home a broken person. How could I go on? My marriage was in shambles; I couldn't think of a single friend except Edna on whom I could count; emotionally I was at rock-bottom; spiritually I knew nothing but pretense and hypocrisy. I really wanted to die. There was nothing to live for, except, of course, the children. Depressed as I was, though, I felt they would be better off without me—I had failed so miserably at everything.

In my manic-depressive state, I even suspected Jim of being unfaithful to me. As soon as I could, I went to Edna's to have a reading. For a long time I had wanted to ask her if Jim was running around on me, but I was too proud to admit to the possibility.

Or was it that unwritten, unspoken, but well-established fear among astronaut families that marital difficulties, unless kept under wraps, automatically disqualified a guy from getting a flight? Frequent rumors circulated throughout the tight little Nassau Bay inner sanctum of extramarital capers involving some of the men when they were away from home. None of us were so naive as to doubt the existence of the eager and available females flirting with our husbands and impressed out of proportion with these celebrated supermen.

Again, Edna was vague in response to my direct question about Jim. This only substantiated my suspicions, and when I couldn't pin her down, I told her I was going to leave Jim. She begged me not to act impulsively, assuring me that the present celestial arrangement would soon be out of conjunction and things would be better. She also told me that if I walked out on Jim now, he never would take me back. So I stayed.

Meanwhile, I continued wrestling with the question I had faced at Claire's funeral. It was as if my dead brother rose up periodically and asked me, "Mary, what are you going to do about it? If you don't settle your soul's destiny, we'll never see each other in eternity." Oh, how I wanted to settle it. But I didn't know how. I groped and searched for answers. I began reading my Bible to find them.

One day I read something that helped relieve my anguish over Claire's death and end my persistent "Why, God?" It said: "The godly die before their time . . . no one seems to realize that God is taking them away from evil days ahead. For the godly who die shall rest in peace" (Isa. 57:1-2).

That was a beginning, but only a faint one, for I couldn't find other answers. As a matter of fact, things only got worse between Jim and me. I decided to pursue my search for spiritual fulfillment in my old church, which only made Jim angrier. But I really didn't know where to start, and it seemed to me that anyplace was better than no place. Jim did not agree and forbade me to take the children. "I don't want them to be as mixed up as you are," he once said bitterly. So I got up early Saturday mornings and left as soon as I prepared breakfast, returning home around 1:00 P.M. to fix lunch, and as soon as possible afterwards went to bed for a long afternoon nap. The next morning, Sunday, Jim repeated the process for the children and himself.

I was well aware that Jim's complaints were valid. He had only the weekend to be home, and because of my stubborn insistence on observing Saturday instead of Sunday with him, we had no time together as a family. Consequently, we spent the two days arguing, pouting, pulling the children between us, or playing the silence game. Hardly a satisfactory way to nurture a marriage or family.

But childhood training, right or wrong, is hard to overcome, and I couldn't easily unlearn the strict teachings of my parents during my formative years. Neither could Jim understand or adapt.

So we were caught in a hopeless deadlock. The tension became so unbearable that we no longer restrained ourselves in front of the children and openly engaged in verbal barrage at the slightest provocation. Always before we had waited until the children were safely asleep, or Jim would refuse to speak and no argument was possible. Now we didn't care. I knew the children were suffering emotionally and were afraid we would do what we threatened— either kill each other or divorce.

I also suspected that Jim was seriously considering giving up his dream-of-a-lifetime opportunity. Chosen for the prime crew of Apollo 15, he was entering an intensive two years of preparation and training. He was so totally absorbed, night and day, that even he described himself as a walking, living, breathing automaton. Of course, I should have been caught up in the glory of it all, smiling and rejoicing in my husband's successes and standing at his side with the support he needed. But I couldn't do it. Nothing in me provided the necessary resources to be what I knew I should be. Or to create the home atmosphere Jim needed to fulfill his lofty aspirations.

After faithfully adhering to the impossible NASA image all this time, I began to realize that being an astronaut's wife meant being almost a nonentity. When the glitter faded and I could see clearly, I began to rebel against the NASA dos and don'ts, the loneliness, the fears and doubts, responsibilities for home and children, cars, plumbing problems, dentists, doctors, illnesses, and the maelstrom of trouble and confusion this misdirected life style imposed upon me. That Jim was a victim as much as I was, I never doubted—but the black cloud was becoming so impenetrable that I finally reached the point where I didn't care about the stupid NASA image. I didn't want to be an astronaut's wife anyway, so why should I continue to let it destroy my life and the lives of my husband and children?

If I could have looked at anything objectively, I suppose the whole scene would have appeared as ludicrous and absurd as it really was. I became deeply involved in church activities, even taught a youth group. At church I was the smiling, everything's great, delightful wife of an astronaut, bearing up triumphantly under the strain of an antagonistic husband who forbade the children to accompany me. At home I dropped the happy mask and assumed the role of a bitter, complaining, retaliating wife.

Eventually my duplicity and hypocrisy caught up with me, and I realized I could not continue this course and remain mentally balanced. That the scales might already be tipped in the wrong direction became a worrisome fear—probably for Jim as well as me.

Already I had weathered another severe emotional shock. Just six months after Clarie's death, my brother-in-law Ernie, who had called to tell me about Claire, was dead. I began to realize that life was one bitter crisis after another, with no apparent pattern or explanation.

One summer morning while the children were outside playing, I washed and set my hair and began cleaning the house. While absentmindedly pushing the vacuum about the living room carpet, my mind seemed weighted as I brooded over the hopeless set of circumstances staring at me. This house I was cleaning, whose every detail I once loved, had now become a loathesome prison. I was trapped in a turmoil of unsolvable problems with no place to turn. The future-predicting astrology I had trusted to clear the maze only thickened it; religion and church attendance were fine while I was there, but I merely returned to the same misery I left and couldn't apply the exalted principles set forth.

I began to stare out the window onto the lovely little courtyard of bright flowers, lush green grass, and beautiful rocks and garden beds. Hot tears of self-pity started flowing. I switched off the vacuum, sat down on the sofa, and kept mulling over the events of the past few months. *Do I want to continue living like this? Is it worth it? Why should I go on? Why should I fight Jim any longer? Why not give up and let him have his way?* As our problems grew distorted and insurmountable in my mind, I became inwardly frustrated, fatigued, and wearily lay down on the sofa. *Jim doesn't love me anyway, so why should I care about anything?* Subconsciously aware that I was still staring emptily into space, I slipped into a mental trance. As I lay there, I gave up hope and totally withdrew from my surroundings.

I wasn't even frightened that the mental imbalance I had feared might now be upon me. After fighting a losing battle for so long, it seemed comfortable to relax my grip and simply give up. It was so comfortable indeed, that I never wanted to return to reality again.

I have no idea how long I stayed there in that state before the children came in. I was completely aware of their presence, and yet I wasn't. I knew they were asking me questions which I didn't answer. Or was it that I couldn't? Though I could hear and knew what was going on around me, I couldn't enter into it—as if I were present, but completely disconnected on the inside.

The children became alarmed. Jill thought I was dead and began crying. Joy assured her I was not. After trying every method they could devise—begging, pulling at me, crying—finally they hit upon scheming. They plotted to do all the forbidden things they could remember, thinking I would become alarmed enough to intervene. It was a strange feeling not to care about anything. When I gave up hope and the will to fight, something inside me turned off, and I was powerless to switch it back on again.

The phone rang. Though I heard it, it seemed far away in another world. Nothing in me stirred. I learned much later that Joy had called my friend, DiAnne and kept saying that something was wrong with her mama. When DiAnne asked her what, she just kept saying over and over that I was lying on the sofa and wouldn't talk or get up. Joy was terrified and begged her to come over. It was then DiAnne decided to call my number hoping to stir me to answer. When I didn't answer, she called NASA and got a doctor for me.

The doctor must have known at a glance what was taking place, for rather than treating me medically, he immediately tried to bring me back by slapping my face, talking, threatening. When I didn't respond, he found a neighbor to keep the children, picked me up like a limp dishrag, carried me to his car, and drove to NASA. All the NASA doctors were well instructed to keep unfavorable publicity as quiet as possible, so if I could be treated out of the eye of the press and eager public, both ready to pounce on any crumb of sensationalism, it would be better. for the space program and Jim.

In case of drug consumption, they pumped my stomach. I had not eaten all day, so it was a ghastly process of gagging and choking. But strangely enough, the entire wretched procedure only affected my body—while I, the real I, remained totally detached and untouched. Whatever they did to my body, they couldn't touch me, and in one sense I felt free for the first time in years. Free from the crushing load, free from the weight of too much responsibility, free from trying to move things in the right direction and failing time after time. Now I could rest.

Finding nothing in my stomach, Dr. McGee began asking a myriad of questions. Again I heard, but I didn't hear. Only my limp body and glassy-eyed stare met his queries. After his many futile attempts to rouse me, suddenly, out of that other world, one word became distinguishable. I struggled to shut it out, but it wouldn't leave. At first it was faint, but it became more insistent, more demanding of my conscious attention. *Jim . . . Jim . . . Jim . . . Jim.* Then I heard it. "I'll have to call Jim." Still I couldn't move, but I felt tears slowly trickle down the side of my face. The doctor saw them too, and he knew he had touched the fountainhead of my river of sorrow.

Now a gentleness replaced the force and pressure, and he began patiently, almost fatherlike, asking if something was bothering me and did I need to talk about it. Still no response. Only tears. If I had known how many other wives kept these doctors busy with vague complaints never quite susceptible to cure, perhaps I could have unburdened my weary heart. But I didn't know. I thought I was all alone. And I was ashamed.

At length, a NASA ambulance drove up, they wheeled me into it and drove to the Methodist Hospital in Houston, thirty minutes away. As soon as Dr. McGee checked me in and briefly instructed the nurse in charge, he left. Then a neurologist appeared to examine me, listening to my heartbeat, checking my pulse, testing reflexes, probing here and there. Finally he turned away and in a tone of disgust for having wasted his time said, "Why in the world was I called? She doesn't need me. She needs a psychiatrist."

Now two fears sharply penetrated my self-imposed shell. First, I feared they would call Jim whom I did not want to see. In fact, I never wanted to see him again.

The neurologist had dropped the second one on me. *He says I need a psychiatrist. He thinks I'm crazy. Maybe I really am. Maybe I didn't just give up hope and withdraw—maybe I lost my mind and they're going to send me to a mental institution for the rest of my life. I had better start talking or I may be in real trouble.*

# No Way to Go But Up

The seventh floor psychiatric ward at Methodist Hospital would have depressed the brightest, most optimistic of souls. After the neurologist had exploded his bombshell on me, a psychiatrist appeared to take me up to the seventh floor in a wheelchair and check me in. If he asked questions or examined me, I can't remember. By now my emotional state was thoroughly shattered, and I didn't want to see anyone. I hadn't wanted to in the first place.

"I'm so tired. Please let me sleep," I pleaded with the first nurse who approached me. Much to my relief, they asked no questions, immediately put me to bed, and gave me a strong sedative. Totally exhausted both emotionally and physically, I wanted to sleep forever. I was oblivious to the passage of time, and when they began to rouse me, I resisted. It seemed I had been asleep only a moment.

As I struggled into consciousness, I became aware of a voice screaming, "No, no no!" Over and over I heard it. I looked around my room, but only an impatient nurse was there. Later I learned it was the girl in the room next to me violently objecting to shock treatments she was forced to receive.

More sleep was not on the agenda for me, and they began pumping pills and questions at a rapid pace. Questions like *Do you think people are plotting against you? Do you hear strange voices? Do you have trouble urinating? Do you resent your father? Do you hate your mother?* Foggy though my mind was, I recognized a sequence and sameness to the questions no matter how disguised they were. So I was careful to be consistent in my answers. On and on it went; I thought they would never stop. When one interrogator disappeared, another would appear and begin all over again.

Between questions, I tried to sleep or read a book I had found on that first day of confinement. With my book propped up during one of those intervals, I sensed the presence of another person and looked up to see Jim standing awkwardly at the door. He hesitated, as if he didn't know whether to come in or remain where he was. I said nothing, just stared at him blankly. All emotion was drained from me.

At length he walked over to my bed, looked down unsmiling and expressionless, and managed to say, "What are *you* doing here? It should be *me*."

"You're right. It should," I cruelly agreed.

We had little to say to each other. I still didn't want to see him, and certainly I had no desire to explain anything. We were like total strangers who had nothing in common. After he left, I reflected upon our mutilated relationship. I kept asking myself, *How is it possible that two people could live together for so long and know one another so little? How could two who once loved each other so much have drifted so utterly apart.* It seemed incredible.

Only twice during my week of hospitalization did I see the psychiatrist, and that was more than enough for me. He seemed so impersonal, so antagonistic, so set upon disturbing me. What I needed was rest and tranquillity. He kept looking at his watch as if he begrudged every second he was forced to give, which further annoyed me. The crowning blow came when he began to probe into my involvement with astrology. He first asked about Edna in a critical way, so I had to rise to her defense. Then he insinuated I had gone off the deep end in dependence on astrology. With that I refused to speak another word, turned my head to the wall, and inwardly seethed. *Who told him I had been consulting an astrologer? If I find out that Jim did, he'll be even sorrier than he is already.*

The nurses began to insist I go to therapy. Again I grew angry and screamed at them, "Go away! I'm tired, and I want to sleep. I didn't come up here to weave baskets." It never occurred to me that what appeared as over-aggressive, rude demeanor on the part of doctor and nurses might merely be spontaneous reaction to my behavior. I had become so totally introspective, selfish, and self-seeking that nothing mattered except my demands. I couldn't see anything in perspective, only as related directly to me. I cooperated with no one.

About the second day I decided to walk around the ward.

Certainly it was not to visit with anybody. I had no desire to talk. I only wanted to get out of the tiny cubicle whose walls seemed to be moving in on me.

Never will I forget the glassy-eyed, vacant expressions of the patients shuffling aimlessly or sitting dejectedly staring at walls or into space. The hopelessness and despair written upon their faces haunts me still. They were alive, but they had given up on life and had removed themselves far from its complexities.

I found a chair, and for awhile studied those pathetic figures. *What circumstances could possibly have driven them to such despondency?* My mind was moving slowly from the effect of drugs given me around the clock. Like I had cement in my brain. *I wonder if those people are drugged also?* I looked up to see a girl staring through a window from a room whose doors were barred. Frightened, I shuddered and quickly got up out of my chair, moved down the hall and out of sight. Wandering around I spotted a little room that was empty except for a piano. I was able to play a few simple hymns which brought a measure of peace to my troubled spirit.

About my third day they brought in a new girl who had overdosed on drugs. I learned that her despondency was over the fact that she was pregnant though unmarried. Immediately I knew I had to see her and do what I could to help. For years I had kept my own secret carefully and painfully hidden, afraid somebody might find out or guess, but now I knew I must tell it. "Don't be afraid to have your baby," I patiently encouraged this poor distraught soul. We spent a long time talking together that day, and when I left, I had the worthwhile feeling of having helped somebody just a little.

Except for an occasional trip to the piano, for the rest of the week I stayed close to my room. To see those shells of people out in the halls and lounges so unnerved me that I couldn't bear to look at them again. *Suppose I reach such a state and become one of them? What then?* I was in no condition to handle this prospect. My only alternative was to isolate myself in my bleak, solitary room to read or sleep. Most of the time I slept, my favorite escape mechanism.

The psychiatrist who was too busy to see me, and whom I didn't want to see anyway, released me to Jim exactly eight days from the time I entered Methodist Hospital. The doctor insisted I continue indefinitely with the tranquilizers and other drugs he felt necessary to a total recovery. So Jim took me home.

The children were excited to see me, but just walking into that house, scene of so much grief, had a chilling effect upon me. Nothing had been resolved through the trauma I had just endured, and I was returning to the same desperately hopeless predicament I had left. The keen edge of my emotions was dulled by the numerous pills I consumed, but the burdensome weight was still bearing down on me, crushing any hope of change. Weary of my plight, I just wanted to sleep, wishing I could awaken and discover it had all been a bad dream—or not awaken at all. The latter course seemed, more and more, the only way out.

Before leaving the hospital, Jim had asked the doctor if he could take me to the King Ranch in Granby, Colorado. Indeed, it would be good for me, the doctor said. So Jim packed the children and me into the car and headed for the mountains he knew I loved best, hoping for a miracle.

July in the Rocky Mountains cannot be described—it has to be experienced. Leaving Houston's stifling humidity, swampy flatness, and depressing gray skies, I wondered if the mountain paradise etched in my memory was real. Perhaps the intervening years with their accompanying sorrow had glorified my mental recollection. But it was just as I had lovingly remembered, only far better with the dimensions of hearing as well as seeing rushing streams tumbling over glistening boulders, soft breezes flipping aspen leaves and waving pine boughs, the chorus of birds gliding overhead, the smell of pine and cedar, of fresh earth, of wood burning in the large open fireplace, of fragrant wild flowers covering the meadows. *Oh, if I could just recapture what I lost moving to Houston,* my heart cried out. *But I'm so tired. I haven't the strength to reach for it—or hope for it—or even desire it, I'm afraid. It's too late,* I concluded.

This was Jim's final effort to salvage our marriage and home, I strongly suspected. The King Ranch, owned and operated by wealthy John King, was an ideal place for that purpose. King was a friend of the astronauts and extended an open invitation to any of them to be his guests at this fabulous dude ranch. It was merely a matter of calling to let him know when we would arrive.

The children had a glorious time riding horses, swimming, bowling, fishing. Jim was with them much of the time, while I spent the days resting, walking, thinking, reading, and being alone. I wanted it that way. We managed to have one family outing—a night of camping out not too far from the ranch.

As long as there was a minimum of involvement and I could be alone much of the time, things went smoothly. But on Friday night Jim and I had a miserable scene.

During my religious quest to find inner peace I had become a vegetarian, had stopped wearing cosmetics and make-up of any description, and had resolved to keep the Sabbath meticulously, so I refused to eat meat that evening or to participate in the gala after-dinner activities.

True to the NASA public image, Jim had carefully concealed our marital discord. Spoiling the image now was bad enough, but with the added strain of this religious conflict that had always come between us, Jim reacted violently. I cried hysterically, we both hurled cruel accusations, and it ended bitterly with my assertion that I could not go on and a divorce would be forthcoming. Jim then informed me this would be the end of his brilliant astronaut career, and he hoped I was happy, because I was to blame.

Huddled outside the bedroom door, the children were listening to our angry exchange. When they heard me say, "I'll take Jill and Jan, and you can have Joy and Jimmy," one of them began to cry.

Any ground we might have gained during the week was promptly lost that Friday night. Now I was sure Jim was deliberately trying to drive me insane so that he could take the children away and put me into an institution. With that thought, the question of the psychiatrist flashed through my mind—*Do you think people are plotting against you?* My brain reeled as it raced from one possibility to the other. *Was Jim plotting against me? Or was I really losing my mind?* I couldn't be sure at this point. Those hopeless, staring faces at the hospital rose from my subconscious and came into focus once again. *Oh, no, no, dear God, no! Please don't let that happen to me.*

Thus ended our week at King Ranch, and all conciliatory attempts washed down the drain. I meant what I said though. I even had the name of an attorney who had counseled with a friend during her divorce ordeal, and my mind was set upon calling him.

Jim could not take longer than a week from his demanding training for Apollo 15's flight, and I was not even close to being ready to return to the Houston scene, so Jim called my friend Virginia in Colorado Springs and arranged for the children and me to stay in a little house adjoining hers on Cheyenne Boulevard. A separation might clear the air for both Jim and me. But I never changed my mind about the divorce. There simply was no other way.

Virginia was good medicine for me. Fun-loving, happy, carefree, a total extrovert, she crammed us all—her two children, my four, and the two of us—into her car for wonderful trips to the mountains, to nearby Canyon City, and to all the places that had been dear to my heart while living in Colorado. Much of the time I was not good company, and I knew it. Morose and withdrawn, it must have been a drag for Virginia, but it it was, she never let on. For a whole month she gave herself freely.

When finally I returned to Houston, I was a bit more rested, but nothing had changed. I still planned to call the attorney and file for a divorce. I even told Jim one night that the next morning I would be calling and arranging for the much-discussed legal action. As usual, he was noncommittal, and, as usual, I was furious. Why I didn't call, I'll never know. I fully intended to, and ordinarily nothing deterred me when my mind was set. The only explanation had to be a mysterious, unseen plan of which I was hopelessly ignorant, but which operated just the same.

Day after wretched day I plodded on, miserably empty and with nothing to live for, merely going through the motions of keeping a house functioning. A house, but not a home. Jim and I avoided each other as much as possible, having learned that a minimum of contact diminished the explosive possibilities.

Whenever we did have an argument, one of us would sleep on the sofa. Much of the time I was the one to move out of the bedroom, and I always hated those nights. The sofa was uncomfortable, so I slept fitfully and awakened about as refreshed as if I hadn't slept at all. The entire day was a lost cause, and I was cross as a bear, which only added to our conflict.

It was a strange paradox. Our incompatibility in the beginning had seemed to center around Jim's absence from the home and my inability to accept the demands of his work. Now his absence was all that kept us together. If he had been home seven days instead of two, we never could have made it. I hated my life with him, but I also hated the thought of being without him. Often I wanted to walk away from the whole scene and never look back, but I couldn't bring myself to do it.

We tried a marriage counselor, but that was no help. I thought Jim refused to be honest with himself, and he thought I overreacted. Neither of us was mature enough to realize that the important issue was *not* who was right or who was wrong. We spent all our energies trying to prove the other wrong. If we had recognized that affixing

94

blame does not solve problems and that solving our problems was, after all, our primary concern, we might have made progress. But we were hung up on this right and wrong thing and couldn't move beyond it.

We managed to make it through another Christmas, giving lavish gifts to the children and each other. Jim gave me a mink stole that year. It was as if we were trying to cover up the emptiness of our home and mend the relationships through superficial means. We didn't know what else to do.

During the next few months a book, *Mirages of Marriage*, fell into my hands. Guilt was again eating away at me, so I tried to read the book with open mind, and a faint glimmer of hope rekindled. Communication between Jim and me had died long ago, so it was a major undertaking even to muster enough courage to speak of the book. Haltingly and apologetically, I tried to discuss what I was reading. But there was no response from him, so I gave up immediately and pushed my festering wounds a little deeper.

As each month came and went, the fact that we were still together surprised both of us. Although it never entered our conversation, little as there was of it, it began to appear that we might make it until after the Apollo 15 flight. My competitive spirit demanded at least that, for I never wanted it said that I forced Jim out of the astronaut program and ruined his career as well as his marriage. Besides, since he was the hero, I was sure to be blamed for the whole rotten mess.

In spite of everything, however, I came to the end of my endurance once again. Weary of the silence, of living in my own world tightly shut out to Jim, of constantly guarding lest I initiate an outburst that would emotionally wreck me for days, of longing for love and tenderness and understanding, I was ready again to file for divorce. This time I actually made an appointment to see a lawyer.

Somewhere I had read that a sensible way to arrive at a decision is to make two lists. So while waiting for my appointment day, I carefully ruled a large sheet of paper and designated the headings: reasons for staying—reasons against staying. Upon completing the list, I counted twenty-six reasons *against* staying, while only one appeared under the reasons *for* staying. That single entry ultimately caused me to cancel my appointment and try a little longer. I simply wrote "It might work." Remote as it seemed, if there was any chance that this marriage might work, my children deserved it.

# Crossing Barriers

I was taking a nap one relaxed April afternoon while the children were outside playing. Suddenly I was jolted into consciousness by eleven-year-old Joy screaming in my ear, "Jill's dead! Oh, mama, Jill's dead! Come quick! Come quick!" I jumped straight up, grabbed my robe, and raced outside. Jill was indeed lying flat on the ground and not breathing. Between gasps and sobs, I finally pieced together what had happened. Jill was climbing a huge tree in our neighbors' yard and had almost reached the top when she lost her footing and fell the distance of two stories, screaming all the way to the ground. Then she became limp and quiet and stopped breathing. Terror filled the eyes of her brother and sisters and all the children standing in a circle looking down on her.

When I felt her warm body, instinctively I knew she was not dead but needed immediate attention. Carefully Joy and I carried her into the house, and I called a NASA doctor who sent an ambulance immediately. Just as they loaded Jill and had closed the rear door, Jim drove up after a two-week TDY exercise, jumped into the ambulance, and rode to Methodist Hospital with them. After treatment and a day of rest, Jill was her bubbly, energetic, tree-climbing self again, except for a broken collarbone.

I was curious as to Jim's first reaction when he drove up and saw the ambulance, so I asked him. I was right. He thought I had had another breakdown and was being taken to the hospital. And I couldn't have blamed him for arriving at that conclusion, for I stayed in a constant state of imbalance and frustration.

As the time drew nearer for Jim's flight, I decided the children had better be prepared, or the life and death aspect of it might prove too traumatic. On April 11, 1970, we took them to see the launching

One of Mary's modeling shots, taken before her marriage to Jim.

Mary's family: Front row (left to right): Jean, Kate, Mom, Donna, Lorraine. Back row (left to right): Claire, Mace, Mary, Dad, Paul, Art, Jim.

The Jim Irwin family in 1965 (left to right): Jill, Mary, Jimmy, Jim, Jan (on Jim's lap), and Joy.

Mary and Lurton Scott immediately after Jim and Dave had landed on the moon.

Mary working on scrapbook of news clippings during Jim's flight.

Jimmy and Jan making a scrapbook for a children's hospital.

Visiting the control center at NASA during the flight. Left to right: George Lowe, Lurton Scott, her mother, Mary, Neil Armstrong, Dr. Gilrath from NASA. *(NASA)*

Mary outside the NASA museum during
Jim's flight.

A welcome home for Jim as he returns from space flight. *(UPI)*

Mary at NASA control center during the Apollo 15 flight.
*(NASA)*

Jim steps off the plane into Mary's arms after his return from Apollo 15 flight, August 8, 1971, Ellington AFB, Texas.     (*AP Wirephoto*)

The returning astronauts give brief speeches to "welcome home" crowd immediately after landing at Ellington AFB, sharing the spotlight with their children.
Left to right: Dave Scott, Merrill Worden, Al Worden, Joy, Jim, Jan, Jimmy, Jill.     (*UPI*)

Lurton and Mary listen to their husbands relate their three days of moon exploration at a press conference.
*(AP Wirephoto)*

Jim and Jan at the airport in Amman, Jordan.

The Apollo 15 crew take a day off for relaxation in Bled, Yugoslavia, before returning home from world tour. *(E. Selhaus)*

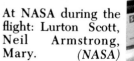

At NASA during the flight: Lurton Scott, Neil Armstrong, Mary. *(NASA)*

Mary, Jimmy, and Jim at the home of Prince Hussein, brother of King Hussein, in Jordan. *(Hagop Toranian)*

The Apollo 15 astronauts receive the Peace Medal, August 24, 1971. Left to right: Lurton and Dave Scott, Secretary of the U.N., U-Thant, Al Worden, George Bush, Mary and Jim Irwin.

Mary and Jim enjoy a sleigh ride in Yugoslavia during world tour.
*(E. Selhaus)*

The High Flight logo.

World Evangelism Foundation crusade rally at Capetown, South Africa. Left to right: "Brother Bill" Rittenhouse, Jill, Mary, Jim.
*(Jim DeNecker)*

Mary and Madalene Harris (right), working
on the manuscript.        *(Leroy Padgett)*

Mary during the flight.

Jim and Mary share a happy moment.

of Apollo 13. Although Jim and I had witnessed several previous launches, I experienced anew through the children's eyes the inspiring exhilaration, the tingling excitement and thrill of the space miracle. Carefully I watched their expressions and noted their comments. When the capsule drifted out of sight, Jill sighed and with dreamy eyes said, "I can't believe I saw that." Jimmy was more practical. "The kids at school'll never believe me when I tell 'em I saw that!"

Standing there on the platform amid a rather awed and hushed crowd, we couldn't know that Apollo 13 would end in near disaster. Astronauts Jim Lovell, Jack Swigert, and Fred Haise didn't know either as they were hurtling into space that an oxygen tank would blow up in the service module just behind the command and lunar modules linked to them. For three anxious days the disabled Apollo 13 would circle the moon using stored power from the lunar module and finally would coast back to earth. The miracle we thought we saw at the launch pad proved to be a far greater miracle than we anticipated. It also proved to be excellent preparation for the children in case a future mishap occurred.

Apollo 14 was scheduled for January 31, 1971, my thirty-third birthday, and Apollo 15 would follow on July 26 of the same year. We were heading down the homestretch with only months for our marriage to last before Jim's flight.

It turned out we weren't the only couple holding a marriage together before a flight. Although I wasn't aware of it, which reveals how little we know about other people, our neighbors, Ed and Louise Mitchell, were putting up a brave front until after Apollo 14's splashdown of which Ed was lunar module pilot. Immediately after the shouting was over and Louise had appeared before the press, TV cameras, and clamoring public to say how proud she was of her husband, she packed her bags and the marriage was over.

But could *we* last? I wasn't sure. It was touch and go whenever Jim was home, and there were often bad scenes, harsh words, wounded feelings, and long periods of silence.

Absent-mindedly turning the car radio dial one day while searching for soothing music to calm my frayed nerves, I heard an appealing song that made me stop and listen. One line stayed with me—"He touched me and made me whole." Tears began to flow, and I really couldn't understand why. Some sort of responsive chord had been brushed, perhaps my desperate longing to be whole and not knowing where to turn, though I had tried everything I knew. Then a man began to tell about his life, how he had reached rock bottom, the end of everything, and had turned to Jesus Christ who had lifted him from his pit of despair. Every word he spoke seemed to describe my condition, for I knew I was at the bottom. I was so moved by what I had heard that I set one of my radio push-buttons on that station so I wouldn't lose it.

I began looking forward to taking the children to their various activities and all the daily errands my growing family demanded, just so I could listen to that station. The deep hungering within me kept me hanging onto each word, each song. Almost every day a recording of Ethel Waters singing "He's All I Need" was played. I eagerly looked forward to hearing that song. Another one was J. T. Adams and the Men of Texas singing "We've Come This Far by Faith." I even bought that record album so I could memorize the words and sing along with them.

The first program I had heard the day I *accidentally* flipped my radio dial was called "Unshackled." As I became a more regular listener, I noticed this was a weekly presentation, so I began to schedule that particular program into my week as if it were an important appointment. Indeed, it was the most important appointment of my life. My heart was hungering and thirsting, and what I heard fed and refreshed me as nothing ever had. Each program featured the story of somebody who told about emptiness and despair and a broken life and how they had found a new beginning, a new life with healing for their wounds and a solution to their hopeless dilemma. I seemed able to relate to all these stories on a deep level. It was like a draught of pure fresh air to a drowning person, and I had been drowning for a long time.

Even though these people told exactly how their lives changed when they found the reality they were seeking, I couldn't seem to get it into my own life. I wanted it. God knows I wanted it. But I didn't know how. I had tried religion, church. But this was different. I knew it was different. And it eluded me for some time.

Meanwhile, Jim and I continued our struggle. Our marriage vows had declared that "we two shall become one," but we never could figure out which one. So we spent our entire time battling for supremacy. And we were both losers.

As Jim's flight drew nearer and he was under more pressure at work, each weekend he came home in a dark mood, fatigued and withdrawn. The moment he walked in, the air grew tense and relationships strained. Being of an explosive, get-it-all-out-in-the-open," door-slamming temperament, as opposed to Jim's silent, contemplative, private-person nature, one day I had had it! After a screaming bout, I finally shouted, "If you're going to act like a child, I'm going to treat you like one!" With that I slammed the kitchen door, got in my car, and began to drive.

It didn't matter where I went. More and more of late after we argued, I had been escaping by taking the car, driving somewhere to park and listen to my station, crying and praying. This day I drove rather aimlessly, mentally reviewing all the events of my life as I drove. *If I could go back*, I kept asking myself, *what would I do differently? How would I change things?* I honestly didn't know.

Suddenly I looked around and realized I was close to Kemah, the old harbor where the shrimp boats come in on the waterway between Galveston Bay and Clear Lake. It was a warm, windy day and my sketchbook and drawing equipment were in the back seat, so I headed my car toward the docks. A bit of sketching might take my mind off the turmoil raging inside.

The place was almost deserted on this Sunday afternoon. I pulled my car into a lonely spot at the end of the bait and tackle shops, slowly walked toward the water, and sat down on an old log by a shrimp boat tied to the dock. The water was murky, and the wind was slowly blowing crumpled and torn paper everywhere. Discarded bottles, old scraps of wood with rusty nails half embedded, and a varied assortment of trash littered the area. I began to sketch. First an old bottle, then a piece of wood with two bent nails protruding. As I was sketching and thinking, I reflected—*This looks like my life. Aimless. Worthless. Blown about.* It seemed so useless. Then I thought about those people from "Unshackled" and remembered how their lives had been like mine. But something had happened. They were changed. How?

Sitting amid the debris, I looked up in desperation and cried out, "God, my life is just like this garbage. It's worth nothing. Who am I? Why am I here? Where am I going? Do something with my life. *Please do something!*" In that moment I realized I had been trying to do it all myself when all the time I was helpless.

Then a strange thing happened. In my mind, like on a big TV screen, I saw two wrestlers. I realized clearly that Satan was one of them and Jesus the other. They were wrestling over my soul. I sat there for what seemed like a full fifteen minutes with my eyes turned inward watching the scene. When the match was over and I saw Jesus with His arm raised in victory, I knew the battle for my soul was won.

I bowed my head and quietly said, "Lord Jesus, if my life was worth fighting for, I will follow You to the ends of the earth. I don't know what that song means, *We've come this far by faith*, but I intend to find out. Help me, Lord, to live the kind of life You fought to win."

I didn't know what had happened, I couldn't have explained it, but immediately I knew everything was changed. I felt cleansed. I felt washed on the inside. My heavy heart was light and free. I could sing again. Oh, I could hope again. Now I understood what they were talking about on the radio. As long as I tried in my own strength to change my life, to do better, to be better, nothing happened. But the moment I turned away from myself and my hopeless condition and looked only to God *knowing I could not do one thing to help myself,* the miracle occurred. It's called faith. Always before it was self-effort—trying, trying, trying, but never achieving. I even tried to produce faith. I believed all the things one is supposed to believe, but it was merely an intellectual grasp of spiritual facts. The difference came when I reached the end of my efforts and wholly looked to God in my helplessness.

It seemed so simple now. Why had it taken me so long to understand? Why had I been so slow of heart and dull of mind?

I stayed there perhaps an hour, perhaps longer, thinking and praying, reviewing my life again. Suddenly it was not hopelessness I felt within, and for the first time in my life I was not alone. A warm, soothing, protective Presence engulfed and filled me, and I knew I could face whatever lay ahead. Not in my own strength, however, for I had just come to the end of that. A new strength surged within, and a deep well of joy began bubbling up and overflowing.

*Should I tell Jim? Would he understand? I doubt it. Would he have time to listen? Would he care? I doubt it. Probably I'd better keep all this to myself, and if it's real and lasting, he'll notice without my telling him.*

Having decided that, finally I rose from the almost sacred log seat where I had come face to face with God and slowly made my way back to my car. But I was not the same person who had despondently shuffled to the spot a few hours earlier. Everything seemed different. Even the trash and offensive odor didn't bother me. I had never liked the Houston area, but today everything was beautiful. My whole world was filled with peace and joy and beauty. I was different, and I knew it.

> Something beautiful, something good
> All my confusion, He understood.
> All I had to offer Him was brokenness and strife,
> And He made something beautiful of my life.

# The Race Against Space

July 26, 1971, was pressing closer, and the last few months of intensive training for David Scott, Al Worden, and Jim Irwin, the next three men destined for lunar exploration, had begun in earnest.

Jim was gone more than ever now, but he made it a point to call every night. I looked forward to those calls. Over the long-distance wires it was easier to make new attempts at constructing a bridge of communication. We began working hard to build that bridge.

My new life within was clamoring for nourishment and growth. I didn't know for a long time that the Bible says, "When someone becomes a Christian, he becomes a brand-new person inside. He is not the same any more. A new life has begun," but I was experiencing it. Just like the newborn infant who instinctively searches for milk, I was drawn to things that strengthened me and enabled me to understand what was happening on the inside.

I had no one to help me, but as I listened to my radio station with a new awareness of what I was hearing, I discovered two sources. First of all, the Bible became an open book at last. I found a paraphrased, modern language Bible at a bookstore and began to read avidly. It was exciting to meet the characters whose names I had heard all my life, but about whom I knew nothing, and to become closely related to them. No longer were they antiquated, distant, unapproachable, mythological figures, but real people, flesh and bone and blood, heart and soul and spirit. Like Elijah, who was described as "a man of like passions." After I read about him, I could relate to him deeply.

My journey into the Scripture began with the Book of John, and a whole new understanding of the person of God in Jesus Christ opened to me. Buried deeply in my subconscious from my earliest memories was the picture of a stern, exacting, unyielding, uncompromising, Supreme Being who watched and heard everything I did or said and was ready to pounce on me at the slightest provocation. Now I saw a loving Father, concerned with every facet of my being, sorrowing in my sorrows, grieving when I fell, intimately involved in my life. My heart was flooded anew with love for the God who had met me on that waterfront log and heard my feeble cry.

Christian paperbacks were my next discovery. Books became my best friends in those early days of spiritual growth. I desired no better company than my books, and I spent hours reading one after another, gleaning from each priceless insights that gradually, step by step, transformed my defeated, negative outlook.

One of the first books that fell into my hands was *Fascinating Womanhood,* loaned to me by my friend Betty. This book was the real beginning of the healing of our marriage. I began to see where I had made horrendous mistakes. In fact, I could have been dashed to the pit of despair at the staggering number of my foolish, thoughtless, senseless reactions to simple situations if it hadn't been for the practical methods the book outlined for repairing broken relationships. I had nothing to lose that hadn't already been lost, I reasoned, so why not swallow my pride. And it was my pride that was the greatest hindrance to progress. It was hard to admit how wrong I had been, how many mistakes I had made. I couldn't always bring myself to these admissions. When I allowed pride to rule, we inevitably regressed. When I let God deal with my pride and strike it a deadly blow, we moved ahead.

A simple, almost ridiculous-sounding suggestion my new book offered seemed to break down barriers between Jim and me. I began to write little love notes and tuck them into his clothes as I packed for him each week. Foolish as it was, he responded positively and was obviously touched to learn that I really cared for him. It had been a long time since I had been able to tell him I loved him because of all the hostility stored within. It had been a long time since I even *thought* I loved him, let alone told him. So writing it seemed less threatening, and soon I could do it sincerely. I began enjoying this little venture as I saw Jim warm toward me.

In the process of building a new relationship, I discovered some rather unpleasant things about myself. The most difficult to face honestly was that I could not accept Jim as he was. I had to admit in several painful sessions before God that I didn't like Jim—his passive nature, his quiet temperament, his inability to express immediately what he thought about a situation when I put him on the spot, his having to mull over and ponder feelings and reactions before verbalizing, his temper. Some of the very things I most admired in him before we were married now antagonized me to the utmost. And why? The answer was a long time coming, and when it came I had a hard time accepting it. *I wanted to be in control. Things must go my way or not at all. This man must change to suit me or our marriage wouldn't work.*

The reason this insight was so long coming was that whenever I moved even close to touching the truth, immediately my defenses rose. *But, Lord, you know how he acts. You've seen his temper, and you've watched him give me the silent treatment—refuse to discuss a situation with me. I admit I'm usually out of control when I want these discussions, but he doesn't have to clam up.*

God didn't have a chance with me as long as I squirmed out of the accusation and placed the burden of guilt for my behavior upon Jim. No matter how wrong Jim was, not until I recognized that I was responsible *only* for my own actions could I begin to accept Jim just as he was, without alterations. And this didn't happen overnight. The rugged, uphill road to even partial success was paved with dismal failures as well as victories. And the failures outnumbered the victories, especially at first.

Becoming responsible for my own reactions and decisions without blaming Jim, or anyone else for that matter, proved to be difficult. For so long I had played the "poor me" game of always finding a scapegoat—parents, older brothers or sisters, husband, children, NASA, Houston, neighbors—that I had virtually no idea how to honestly approach the routine problems brought on in part by our complicated ultra-civilization. My greatest struggle, I thought, was learning to love and accept Jim anew. With my inability to accomplish this, however, I began to probe a little deeper and was amazed to discover that the root of being unable to love Jim lay in the fact that I didn't really love myself.

Now I was confused. I had always ascribed my selfish, self-centered approach to everything as evidence that I loved myself in excess, never dreaming the opposite was true. Secretly I felt inferior, rejected, worthless, that everybody else was smarter, prettier, more capable, and better than I. But it was too painful to plunge into the sewer of suppressed hostilities and hurts to find out what was down there and, more importantly, why. So I had never bothered. I kept the lid tightly closed, opening it only to thrust into oblivion another wound, another sorrow, another defeat. Out of sight and out of mind meant out of existence to me.

How wrong I was. Everything that had ever happened was carefully stored in that sewer and lay festering and poisoning my whole being. Somehow, if cleansing and healing were ever to occur within me, the whole rotting mess had to be dredged up and exposed to the healing touch of a loving heavenly Father. But I wasn't ready for that yet. So I struggled on trying to draw upon my newfound faith and God's inexhaustible love and patience. And He blessed it. Our marriage relationship began to improve.

Another simple device suggested in *Fascinating Womanhood* was the tool of praise. I couldn't remember the last time I had complimented Jim or sincerely praised him. This was difficult at first, too. Long-standing habits do not crumble easily. It takes effort and consistency. In the beginning, I thought I sounded pretentious, unnatural, insincere. Probably I did. As I began to look for the good and the praiseworthy in Jim, however, I couldn't believe how for-granted I had taken many of his conscious efforts to please me. Like the electronic air-filter he had installed so I could sleep all night without my allergies awakening me. When I saw how delighted he was after each compliment, this in turn rewarded me.

My second reading adventure was the story of Nicky Cruz, *Run Baby Run*. As I read his account of the cruel rejection he encountered at every turn in life, a deep well of responsiveness opened from within me. I hadn't thought much about rejection, and had never identified any of my emotional problems as being the result of early rejection, but coming from so large a family with both parents pressured day and night to provide for the necessities of ten demanding children, it was not inconceivable that number nine could be lost in the shuffle.

I began delving rather deeply into the whole area of rejection—its symptoms, causes, consequences, and cure, and all because the story of Nicky Cruz alerted me to the core of my own emotional malady. The thing that had thrown me off the scent of this elusive culprit was that I *knew* my parents loved me dearly and were devoted to their children, home, and the family unit. How, then, could I accuse them of rejecting one of the children they so obviously loved? I was only thinking, of course, of *overt*, open rejection.

It had never occurred to me that their total preoccupation with duty and consequent lack of time for personal, individual attention had been interpreted in my childish, immature mind as rejection. It did not matter that they loved and adored me. If I was not able to receive their unemotional, distant type of love, if I *thought* I was rejected by my parents, I was.

Gradually I began to understand the emotional barrier between my parents and me that produced guilt whenever I thought about the lack of warmth in our relationship. Gradually, also, I understood that my marriage problems were not centered in trying to love Jim. Because of this early sense of rejection, I could neither give nor receive love. I was still a demanding child, desperately needing love and attention, but unable to receive it. That sense of rejection made me feel unworthy of being loved and programed me for the inferior feelings I had always struggled against. If my parents didn't love me, I had subconsciously reasoned, I wasn't worth being loved. Therefore, I couldn't even love myself. I wasn't good enough. Knowing this helped a little, but altering such deeply ingrained patterns meant the beginning of a long pilgrimage.

Now that a glimmering of hope for the survival of our marriage had appeared, we began to have some good times. One of the first such times was the Apollo 14 launch. Jim was already there, of course, so I arranged care for the children, and Betty and I drove Jim's bright red Corvette from Houston to Cocoa Beach.

Betty was my oldest friend in Houston; we had met almost the first week we moved from Colorado Springs into the Galveston Bay apartment complex. Typical of her uninhibited personality, Betty had walked in one evening before our boxes were unpacked and order established. The place was disorganized and littered, children sitting around the floor eating, and I was infuriated beyond words that this pushy woman should walk right in uninvited and unwanted bringing a loaf of freshly baked bread. I tried merely to stand at the door and receive it, but nobody shuts Betty out when she wants to come in. As humiliated as I was for anyone to see such total disarray, it's a wonder we became friends. But we did—we became close friends—and many times Betty was an antidote to my anxious, guilt-ridden, inhibited disposition.

The details of this particular trip to the Apollo 14 launch must have been divinely arranged. All my memories of driving trips were too traumatic to recall. Fighting children, weary after-midnight packing and cleaning, pressure, utter exhaustion, haranguing, complaining, regulating our stops to little children's needs, losing shoes and misplacing clothes—before too many miles Jim and I were cross as caged lions, yelling at the children and at each other and wishing we'd never set out. No trip was really worth what we went through.

Imagine my surprise to learn that traveling can be enjoyable. Betty drove most of the way while I read to her. We stopped whenever we chose—to eat, to investigate something that looked interesting, to relax at a shady, inviting-looking wayside spot, just whatever we wanted to do. Betty's total lack of inhibition helped me overcome some of mine and relax.

Perhaps the most therapeutic aspect of the entire trip was the deeper insight I gained into Betty's life. Although I knew her well, *I thought*, she had hidden much of her wretched past life from me. Now she opened the tightly locked closet and revealed the ghosts of the past. This laughing, carefree soul, who appeared to have not a burden in the world, struggled under an excruciating load of guilt and failure. Married at fifteen, divorced at eighteen, and forced by a second husband to give up two little boys and never see them again was greater grief than I could imagine. I suppose she shared these secrets only because she longed to see her boys, now grown and living in Florida, on this trip. She had had little contact with them from the time she kissed them good-by as babies and was not even sure they could relate to a mother.

Our visit with them was delightful, but, best of all, it provided an emotional healing for Betty and the boys. The grandmother who raised them had taken every opportunity to ingrain within them a hatred for the mother who ran off and left them. The picture she painted was of an immoral, hateful, wicked, self-centered woman. Both of her sons were openly relieved to find that their mother loved them and that she was not the wretched derelict they had been led to believe. And it helped me to realize that some people had more heartbreaking problems than I did.

Having arrived at Cocoa Beach and the motel room Jim had reserved for us, we were caught up immediately in the endless round of parties and celebrations always accompanying a moon launch—luncheons, important people making speeches, banquets, cocktail parties, brunches. Thousands of people traveled to these historic events, and they were in a gala, holiday mood. Betty and I exuberantly joined them, loving every minute.

January 31, 1971, the day of the launch (also my birthday), dawned overcast, gray, and threatening rain. Disappointment filled the atmosphere. The launch would go on as scheduled, but we would not be able to see through the thick cloud cover. Everybody fervently hoped, and many of us prayed, that the sky would clear.

Famous people were in abundance that day scattered throughout the crowd. Always timid and shy in the presence of celebrities of any description, I usually just stood and stared with everybody else. Not Betty. If she wanted to meet anyone, she'd poke me and say, "Look who's over there. Wanna meet him?"

Close to countdown time, assembled with a large excited group of spectators, Betty, Jim, and I stood watching the sky with drooping spirits as a few raindrops began to fall. A Catholic priest a few yards away shot up a large black umbrella over his head. Betty, a Catholic herself, darted over and disgustedly addressed the short, plump, rather eccentric-looking priest: "Father, what are you doing with your umbrella up?" she remonstrated. "Where is your faith? Don't you know you're standing right next to a Baptist minister who is trusting God for a clear sky?" She stalked back as the poor little man sheepishly put down his umbrella and looked up apologetically at Dr. William Rittenhouse, renowned pastor of the astronauts. "Brother Bill," as he was affectionately called by them, smiled broadly and patted the priest on the back. Then they both laughed.

Our faith was not misplaced, for the clouds parted and the sky cleared just before the crucial moment, and we observed again man's triumph over space.

Learning to pray *with faith* was a new experience for me. I had prayed often before my conversion, but it was always one of those SOS type prayers—*Help! I'm in trouble, and I don't know where else to turn.* There was no faith involved, just a desperate grasping for anything that might alleviate the immediate discomfort. Even as I cried out in anguish, I was never sure where I was calling or whether help would come. I only knew that everything else had failed. So why not try prayer?

Now I had a compassionate, loving Father who cared more about my needs than I did myself, and I was learning to relate to a family context of warmth and concern. I was learning, also, to reach for God on more than an emergency basis and simply talk with Him, sharing my innermost desires and thoughts with the One who said, "I will never leave you, nor forsake you." As I began to exercise faith—believing without seeing—God answered many of my prayers in amazing, spectacular fashion. Each supernatural answer, like the parting of the clouds so we might enjoy Apollo 14's launch to the fullest, strengthened my faith and gave me the spirit of a little child bringing my needs before a loving father.

*Remembering* to pray when problems arose was my chief obstacle in those early days of learning to walk with God. For thirty-three years I had struggled on my own to work things out. Prayer was only a last resort when all hope was gone. The habit of worry and self-effort was so ingrained that when I finally remembered I could pray instead of worry, it took me by surprise. Long before I knew the Bible said, "You have not because you ask not," I learned it from experience.

Another wonderful change was taking place within me as I learned to pray *in faith.* As I leaned more upon God—sharing deep confidences, telling Him my needs, depending upon Him solely—my grasping, smothering dependence upon Jim lessened. And as I relaxed my hold upon him, he was more free to be himself.

Seven weeks before Jim's flight found us not only together, but with our marriage growing stronger a step at a time. It was with keen anticipation that *together* we looked forward to the pinnacle of Jim's coveted but hard-won career.

Just as soon as the children were out of school in early June for summer vacation, we packed up and headed for Cocoa Beach where Jim had rented an ocean-front apartment for the entire month. It was a beautiful, ultra-modern, white stucco building with large balconies set amid palm trees, tropical plants, and brilliant flowers.

All morning long the children and I played on the beach, dashing in and out of the foaming surf, jumping waves, and often walking miles at ocean edge with cool, wet sand oozing between our toes as we searched for specimens for our shell collection. Each new and different find was as exciting as if we had located buried treasure. Early every afternoon dark clouds began building until the sky was covered and a torrent of rain deluged our ocean playground. Nobody complained about taking an afternoon nap with the rain pounding on our balcony and windows. Best of all, Jim returned from work every evening for supper with his family. It had been years, all the way back to Colorado Springs, since we had enjoyed the luxury of father in the home every evening.

The second weekend of our glorious vacation Jim and I were

invited by friends to fly to the Bahamas. Other friends offered to keep the children so Jim and I could go alone. What a refreshing renewal of mind, spirit, and body! It reminded me of the lovely days in Monterey early in our courtship. Each day was filled with golden moments I knew I would cherish the rest of my life.

Lou, the astronaut's colorful old Navy cook, invited all of us to spend a day on his houseboat the third weekend. The children were excited as he had promised to take us to the big waterways and search out hidden coves. We even explored a small island which, if it hadn't been for a heavy infestation of mosquitoes, would have been a Robinson Crusoe adventure for the children. It might still have been if their mother hadn't pestered them with bug spray and constant warnings about disease-carrying insects.

All too soon our beautiful holiday came to an end, and it was with sadness that we packed our gritty, sandy belongings, loaded the car, and headed home. Jim took off a few days to drive us back to Nassau Bay, but he had to return to the Cape immediately to begin the customary three-week quarantine before Apollo 15's historic flight on July 26.

It was with mixed emotions that I drove him out to the flight line and watched as he and Dick Gordon, Dave Scott's back-up man, filed their flight plan. I knew it would be many lonely nights before we would be together again—five weeks, to be exact. Jim kissed me good-by, I joked with Dick a few minutes, then quickly turned before Jim could see the tears forming in my eyes and ready to spill down my cheeks. I sat in the car and watched as the two of them walked across the open field to their white NASA T-38 jet, unlocked the canopy to put their clothing away, and climbed in. Just before sliding into his chute, Jim turned and waved. I looked at him through a watery blur and whispered, "Hurry back, my darling."

In just minutes they were airborne, and as I watched, it seemed they were shooting straight toward the moon. Contemplating a whole lifetime of good-bys and separations, I looked up into the heavens at the disappearing jet stream and cried aloud, "Oh, dear God, must my entire life be spent saying good-by to the one I love? Will he come back this time?"

Suddenly my newfound faith rose within, and the fear and grief disappeared. Peace filled my heart, and for the first time I knew, *by faith*, that I could trust God for Jim's safe return.

# Shooting for the Moon

Reporters and photographers were everywhere in our usually quiet neighborhood the three weeks before flight time. They reminded me of ants crawling all over with their cameras set up in the street, in our yard, in trees to get shots through our windows. They even sat waiting at our doorways.

For the first few days I was patient and understanding, knowing that Apollo 15 was the biggest news story on the national front and these men were merely doing their job. I spent hours giving interviews, answering all manner of questions, posing for pictures with the children or alone. When the questions became too personal or touched subjects I didn't want to discuss with the whole world, I refused to answer. Undoubtedly this was interpreted by them as a stubborn lack of cooperation, but I got to the point where I didn't care. I just wanted them out of my way.

They took photographs of everything they could think of—the children at play, watching television, drawing pictures of their daddy on the moon. Some they printed turned out to be hilarious, such as the one where I was kneeling in the foreground digging in my garden with three of the children behind me. A baby robin had fallen from its nest and we had been trying to feed it. The caption read:

MRS. JIM IRWIN SEEKS WORMS IN HOUSTON
. . . waiting are children Jan, 6, Jimmy, 7, and Jill, 10.

Soon I lost my patience with the prying, snooping busybodies from the press. It was true they had a job to do, but so did I, and their presence day and night intruded into my necessary routines and privacy and went far beyond, I felt, the ordinary call of duty. When I caught them in the trees surrounding our house so they could get

111

unposed, inside pictures, I kept the drapes tightly drawn. Then I noticed seven-year-old Jimmy with an expensive camera hanging from his neck going about the house taking pictures. When questioned, he said he had been bribed by one of the photographers to take inside shots of all the rooms and family members. It was then I threatened my four children within an inch of their hide if they so much as talked with any stranger in the neighborhood.

A batch of new kittens and painting the inside of the house before leaving for the Cape occupied my time, to say nothing of keeping noisy children busy and fed and out of my hair. During the two weeks just before the flight, I sent Joy and Jimmy to a special camp for children with learning disabilities. Not only would it help them, but it would be blessing beyond description for me to have less confusion in an already over-confused situation.

Added to all this, I really missed Jim and was feeling a certain amount of anxiety over his flight. Jim called every night, and I really looked forward to that time when I could tell him all that had happened during the day, any local news I might have heard, and learn what he had been doing. He assured me he couldn't do much while in quarantine.

At last the long-awaited day for our departure arrived. I had asked Betty to pick the children up at camp, and my widowed sister, Donna, and her son arrived Wednesday before we flew out on a jet Friday afternoon.

It was good to see my sister. So much had happened during the intervening years since we had been together for any length of time—all the way back to the traumatic months I spent with her before Jim and I were married. Donna was not accustomed to the Houston, NASA, or Irwin pace, any one of which would kill an ordinary human being. She and her son lived quietly in a tiny town with only the noise of birds and squirrels. So her undue excitement at the awesomeness of the experience laying ahead of her coupled with the noise and distraction of four children was easy to understand. As for me, it was the only way I knew how to live.

Upon arriving at Patrick Air Force Base late Friday afternoon, I immediately called Jim. He begged me to join him at the beach house where he had been quarantined in a lonely, isolated spot so we could be together one more time before the flight. With Donna to care for the children, I could easily spend the night and be back with the children by morning. With that decided, I called Lurton

Scott, Dave's attractive brunette wife, with whom I would be sharing the national limelight since Al Worden was a bachelor.

During our discussion about what we would wear to the dinner arranged in our honor, I casually mentioned my plans for the night. I assumed she would be spending it with Dave, so I was taken off guard when she said, "Mary, how could you think of doing such a thing? Suppose you are harboring some kind of bug and Jim's life is endangered because of the exposure? The other fellows might not make it either. In fact, the whole flight could be a disaster." Urgently she pleaded, "Don't go! Please don't!"

"I'll think about it, Lurton," I replied.

For three weeks I had not seen Jim. What a decision to make. *Suppose, just suppose, Jim did not come back—and I didn't spend the night with him. Never saw him again. How could I face knowing I had deprived both of us of this one last time together?*

*On the other hand, suppose I did have a latent virus and ruined the greatest opportunity of his life? Could I live with that?*

After much weighing of fact and feeling, my decision to let head rule over heart seemed right, and I called Lurton to tell her. She was greatly relieved, and we began planning our wardrobe for the elaborate festivities in our honor.

Even as we were chatting, I was vaguely aware that my stomach seemed a bit upset, but I brushed it off as excitement, nerves, and the plane trip. Perhaps a little rest would settle it and help me face the long, jubilant evening ahead.

But I didn't get better—only worse. Suddenly a wave of nausea struck me and I rushed to the bathroom, vomiting all the way. *Now my stomach will feel better having rid itself of whatever bothered it, and I'll still be able to go,* I assured myself. The longer I lay waiting for the misery to pass, the more I realized it was not going to pass, and I would never make it to the dinner party. Again I called Lurton and asked her to express my apologies to the host.

All night long I was up and running to the bathroom. By morning I felt I was going to faint and knew I had better call a doctor. Normally, calling a doctor is a simple procedure, but with the press watching my every move, one little slip could cause Jim to be disqualified for his flight. So I called a NASA doctor who had treated me on a previous occasion and whom I felt I could trust. He didn't seem overly excited about my condition, and when he left, I supposed I would be well and up by afternoon with no one the wiser.

He must have found the nearest telephone, for in fifteen minutes a small medical team arrived and began scolding me for not calling the NASA medical headquarters. They took blood and urine samples and began questioning me intensively. *Had I been to see Jim or any of the crew? Was I sure I had not come in contact with them? Had I forgotten any possible time they could have been exposed to this virus?* I was so weak I could hardly wait for them to leave me alone.

*Oh, why did I have to get sick*, I thought self-pityingly, *and ruin my whole trip and all the exciting parties I've looked forward to? I can't even wear the new clothes I bought just for the parties.*

Two of my brothers, Art and Mace, had arrived for the flight, and by Saturday evening I felt strong enough to go with them to see Jim behind a glass. I had promised Jim weeks before that I would take his place at Manned Flight Awareness awards and do autographs for him. Weak and wobbly though I was, I stayed thirty minutes at the awards, then went on to see Jim for a brief time.

Behind that glass wall he looked wonderfully relaxed, deeply tanned, and seemed, in every way, ready for his flight just hours away. Knowing I would not see him again until he landed at Ellington Air Force Base in Houston after the flight, I had to struggle with my emotions to keep from bursting into tears. Ahead of him still were hours of last-minute briefings, physicals, and simulators—so I wanted to display encouragement, not tears and anxiety.

Before returning to our motel room, we decided at Jim's suggestion to circle around to the launch site and see Apollo 15 at close range. Although our room had a view of the spacecraft, and I had drawn back the draperies several times to view the gigantic, thirty-story object from that distance, it appeared no larger than one of my fingers. As I stood beneath it now, its massive, brightly spotlighted marble-white exterior with liquid nitrogen vapors rising heavenward loomed gigantically above me. Watching those vapors slowly ascend, knowing they could be seen only when the rocket was loaded with fuel and ready for flight, I had a strange, empty feeling. Even though Jim had spent the entire years of our marriage traveling, at least I always knew he was still on the same planet. In a little more than thirty hours, he would be on his way to another world, a mysterious, almost unexplored world I could never see. Only six men in all the universe, in all the ages of time, had ever stepped foot on that light of the night.

Although physically spent and weak by the time I crawled into bed, sleep would not come. My stomach churned, not from the virus this time, but from apprehension and fear. So I began to pray. As I poured out my anxious heart to the God who had created and hung the moon in space, an unspeakable peace calmed my spirit. For a long time I lay there looking out the window at the sight of the full moon and marveling at the transformation of my troubled heart by simply lifting it up in childlike fashion to my Father who said, "My peace I give to you." I had been a worrier from my earliest memories, so I never ceased to marvel at the miracle of the transformed heart.

Sunday I lounged around our room so that I would be completely recuperated and able to enter fully into Jim's highest hour. He had always wanted to fly higher than anyone else, and now he was having his chance. He called that night, and we had our last conversation before Monday's launch. Again I lay awake for hours after his call speculating about the lift-off, our future, recalling again the bitterness of our past years, contemplating whether or not it had been worth all the conflict, loneliness, confusion, and fear. Finally I drifted off into a somewhat troubled sleep only to be awakened a little before seven o'clock by a ringing telephone. After hurriedly dressing and gulping down some rather dry toast and weak tea, the children and I, along with Donna, her son, and my two brothers, scurried into a waiting limousine before eight and were driven to our viewing area.

Even though our motel was a comparatively close fifteen-minute drive from the launch site, with the bumper-to-bumper traffic on this historic morning, we barely made it in an hour. The waterways were crowded with boats, beaches jammed, and every conceivable spot occupied. Helicopters flew overhead keeping a hawk-eye surveillance over the readied spacecraft lest anyone should slip in and sabotage the flight. Security could not have been tighter. Without a badge, no one, absolutely no one, entered the guarded area, so we all securely fastened ours during the drive.

A few years earlier NASA had built a special astronaut family viewing area, but with each launch, the number of relatives and friends gathering there increased to the point that Sue Bean was able to see and hear little of her husband's Apollo 12 launch. Remembering the incident, I was determined this would not happen to me, so I arranged for our PIO men (Public Information Office) to seek out a quiet, private spot just for family members of the crew. The one they chose was perfect for viewing. It was a small rise situated immediately beside a bayou, and although it was the prescribed three miles from the rocket, which is the closest NASA allows, it seemed much closer because of the immense size of that 360-foot monster poised and waiting on Launch Pad A.

NASA had spared nothing to make our little spot comfortable and accommodating. A large TV had been installed along with a speaker connected to launch control so we could plainly hear countdown, and Lou, the astronauts' cook, had prepared sandwiches, coffee, punch, and iced tea so we could snack. There were enough chairs for the twenty or so people gathered, but few of them were used. Eager with anticipation, everybody stood around chattering and laughing, and the excitement level steadily rose as we waited for the crucial moment. In addition to Lurton's immediate family and mine, Jan and Neil Armstrong and Mike Collins joined our party. The children played in the dirt or chased each other, while the adults exchanged all the information they knew about space exploration. Neil and Mike were never-ending sources of technical details which made the viewing far more interesting to all of us. No press people or photographers were allowed in to hassle our little group.

Even at nine in the morning it was getting unbearably hot. Hardly a breeze was stirring, and I felt sweaty and sticky as the sun beat down upon us.

Every few minutes Mission Control blared over the loudspeakers, "Everything is go!" Whenever I heard those words, my stomach quavered and my heart beat wildly with anticipation—something like one feels on that first huge descent of a roller coaster.

The last thirty minutes of waiting seemed endless, and it was obvious that everybody else was nervous and anxious as well. At last the final countdown began. At T-minus thirty I climbed onto one of the folding chairs so I wouldn't miss a thing, but I was still weak, and my brother Art held onto me. At exactly 9:34 A.M. as the voice over the loudspeaker cried "Ignition," great clouds of white smoke came belching from the base of the rocket followed immediately by vivid billows of fire mushrooming out of the smoke. The roar of the engines was deafening as the huge bird lifted off the ground slowly at first, gathering momentum every second, and aiming its pointed nose up, up and away towards the rugged mountains of the moon.

116

Although the white-hot tail it spewed was blinding, I couldn't take my eyes off the majestic rocket streaking upward until it disappeared through a thin layer of clouds. As long as I could see it, I felt close to Jim, but when it finally vanished, I felt all alone and wanted to cry. Jim was in that rocket, and all the years and tears of preparation were over. My heart went up with him, and I would not rest until that little capsule parachuted safely into the blue waters of the Pacific.

It would be almost five days before the spacemen would reach their lofty destination and Dave and Jim would climb down a frail ladder into inches of deep lunar dust that had lain undisturbed since creation. Meanwhile, there was nothing further for me to do but pack, return home, and wait. Communication with the spacecraft was automatically switched to Houston as soon as it had cleared the launch tower, so I would have to be there to follow its progress.

Before returning to Patrick Air Force Base and our room, Lurton and I were taken to the Holiday Inn where the press was waiting for a conference. We were growing accustomed to these press sessions and could handle them with more ease now. And after years of "staying by the stuff" and being hidden behind the action, we were elated to share with our husbands the attention of the world. How glad I was that Jim and I had stayed together and could experience together this triumph of a lifetime.

Once home, nothing occupied our minds or time but the space drama. My sister and Jim's parents remained with me during the entire flight, most of the time watching a silent TV and listening to the "squawk box" NASA had installed on the nightstand beside my bed. Every communication from the spacecraft was transmitted into that little box. For several days I was a bit despondent because I didn't hear Jim's voice—always Al or Dave. I began to wonder if Al had accidentally ejected Jim and wasn't telling. In the evenings after the fellows had gone to sleep in the spacecraft, Dick Gordon, Dave's back-up man, came over to tell me all that had transpired during the day. Most of the astronauts spent all day at Mission Control monitoring the flight.

Twice Lurton and I went to Mission Control and sat in the VIP viewing area, but our PR man refused to allow us that privilege during critical times such as lunar landing or lift-off from the moon. Of course we wanted to be there at those times, but they were trying to protect us in case something went wrong.

The day scheduled for lunar landing we all sat glued to the TV and squawk box. Mom and Dad Irwin sat on the bed with me, the children were scattered around the room, and Charlie Duke was sitting on the floor. Charlie was scheduled for Apollo 16 and had been training in the simulator, so he knew exactly what Jim and Dave were seeing. So did I. Jim had taken me on several missions in the simulator, a training device identical in size and instrument panel to the lunar module, so I knew well the terrain of the landing spot. Now we heard Jim's voice constantly as he gave Dave all the computer information for landing. He sounded calm and steady. I watched Charlie's expression. His eyes would light up and the muscles in his hands, arms, and face tensed as they drew nearer to the designated Hadley-Appennines site. We hardly dared breathe for fear we would miss the landing. Suddenly we heard Jim say "Bam," and we knew they had touched down on the moon's surface.

Relief and ecstatic joy flooded my heart as I reached for my Bible and turned to my favorite passage—the Twenty-third Psalm. I read aloud while Jim's mother repeated it from memory with me. "The Lord is my Shepherd, I shall not want. . . ." Grateful tears flowed down my cheeks. When I had finished reading, we all bowed our heads for a brief prayer of thanksgiving. What a triumphant moment this was for me to share the lifelong dream of the man I loved. And after years of doubting and questioning, what a triumph to know assuredly that I did love him.

At first it was hard to imagine that one of those weightless moon-men bouncing up and down on the TV screen could possibly be my husband. I studied them intently trying to determine which one was Jim since they both looked exactly alike. Then we noticed that Dave had a red band around his arm, so we could identify each at a glance.

The Apollo 15 expedition was to be the most scientifically ambitious and productive of all the moon trips thus far. Even the Hadley-Appennines landing site was the most difficult ever faced by astronauts and held the most interest for scientists on earth because it contained mountains, a valley, and craters created by volcanic action. Dave and Jim were scheduled to stay longer and explore more than any of their six predecessors. The little moon buggy, Lunar Rover, which was the first man-driven vehicle ever to roam the face of the moon would be responsible for making this extensive exploration possible. But I knew the unknown dangers of the little

118

buggy too, and until they checked it out and found it operative, we were a bit tense.

Like most earth vehicles, the Rover had a problem—the front-wheel steering did not work. However, after a short test drive, Dave and Jim discovered that it was ready to go with only its back wheels steering. The only other problem I knew about was if the little buggy should break down several miles from their life-supporting spacecraft. Dave and Jim would not be able to thumb a ride to the nearest service station. They would be forced to kangaroo-hop all the way back, trusting that their vital supplies would last. Quickly I thrust that possibility out of my thoughts, refusing to spend the next three days in anguished suspense.

Before I realized it, August 7th, day of the dramatic splashdown and the space heroes' return to earth, had arrived. Lift-off from the moon, leaving the little lunar buggy behind, and docking of the *Falcon* with the mother ship, *Endeavor*, was flawless and allowed us little time for anxiety. The fellows transferred their precious cargo of moon rocks and soil exactly on schedule, climbed into the command module with Al Worden, securely closed the hatches, and undocked their faithful LM *Falcon* so that Houston could fire its engines by remote control and crash it into the surface of the moon.

Just before splashdown, the house was full of friends who had come to watch the dramatic, unbelievably clear, color TV pictures of the event and to celebrate. Mom and Dad Irwin sat with me in our bedroom, and the rest of the party watched and listened to a second TV and squawk box combination in the living room.

The cameras had picked up the spacecraft at least five minutes or so before splashdown, so we saw the beautiful red, white, and blue striped parachutes blossom out, slowing down the hurtling capsule as it swung to and fro. My heart almost stopped beating for a terrifying moment as one chute failed to open. Quickly I closed my eyes and lifted a frantic prayer for their safety, and once again the miracle of the transformed heart occurred instantaneously and I was absolutely calm. A second after I opened my eyes, the craft landed safely in the bright blue Pacific 285 miles north of Hawaii and began bobbing up and down. Sitting on my bed, I began to clap my hands and squeal with delight like a little child.

Almost immediately frogmen in a life raft climbed up, opened the hatch, and three grisly-looking men with a twelve-day beard growth stepped down into the raft. One of them bent over and splashed water on his face. I laughed, for again I knew almost certainly that it was Jim. And I was right, for that was one of the first questions I asked him.

I had invited "Brother Bill" Rittenhouse, pastor of Nassau Bay Baptist Church, and his dear wife Nell for the celebration, so as soon as the waiting helicopter hoisted the men up to transfer them to the USS *Okinawa*, I asked Brother Bill to lead us in a prayer of thanksgiving. "Thank Thee, O heavenly Father, for the safe return of this crew," he began. By the time he finished, he had eloquently expressed the joy and gratitude of all our hearts.

In addition to the squawk box, NASA thoughtfully had installed a special telephone with a large red light that was somehow hooked up to the *Okinawa* and enabled Jim to call the moment he stepped onto the ship. Our conversation was brief, but just to hear his voice again was joy beyond description. He was headed for several hours of intensive physical examinations after his first solid meal in twelve days—steak!

The next evening, Bill Der Bing, our NASA protocol man, drove us to Ellington Air Force Base to meet the crew when they flew in from Hawaii. This was the first crew not required to submit to another three-week quarantine. NASA had learned from previous flights that contamination to earthlings by any mysterious moon bugs was impossible. So we would have Jim home almost immediately.

Before it ever landed, I could see and hear the large aircraft carrying our brave, but weary, spacemen home. Though the hour was late, a little after 9:00 P.M., and it was pitch dark and raining, over a thousand people had gathered to welcome the heroes. Jim and Al emerged clean-shaven, but Dave had promised his two children they could see his beard. As they descended, our four children ran up and almost pushed their space-wobbly father off balance as they embraced him. Then Jim reached over to me, placed a fragrant red carnation lei around my neck, and kissed me lovingly. It was a tender moment for us both.

The three men then climbed a wooden platform and greeted the raincoated and umbrella-holding welcomers, telling the damp crowd how much they appreciated all the help from those who had given so much of their time and how glad they were to be home. Many people wanted to shake hands and congratulate them, of course.

By the time we arrived home and Jim's parents left to spend the night in an apartment arranged by friends, the hour was late. Our exhausted children went willingly to bed. As Jim and I sat alone talking over the past two weeks, a strange feeling came over me. It reminded me a little of Christmas morning. After months of excited preparation and planning, suddenly all that was left was a bare-looking tree and a living room littered with debris.

Now it was over. The pinnacle of Jim's hard-won, long-sought career had been reached, and he was only forty-one years old. Could there be any challenge left for him in life? Or would it all be anticlimactic from here on? Once again fear for our future crept into my heart.

# A Higher Flight

The first night Jim was on the moon, I walked outside into our yard and stared at it for a long time trying to imagine what he must be experiencing. Always before the moon had seemed so far away and inaccessible, but tonight my impression was totally different. As I looked, it became warm and personal and close.

Lying in bed later, I still couldn't turn my mind off even though my body was weary. I kept thinking about Jim up there hundreds of thousands of miles away. As I lay wide awake, I moved in every conceivable position to catch sight of the moon from my bed, but because of the eight-foot fence we had constructed for privacy, it was not visible. Still awake with my mind alive and full of moon imaginings, I decided to pray for Jim, so I climbed out and knelt beside my bed, glancing out the window before beginning. There, to my utter surprise, shone the full moon—*visible only when kneeling*. How excited I was to discover the secret of viewing the moon from my bedroom. Now I could pray with great fervency for my beloved up there prowling its face.

How I longed for Jim and me to grow *together* spiritually, to be able to share what was happening on the inside of each of us. Looking back, I knew Jim was a Christian. That was what he had been trying to tell me that day in Dayton soon after we were married. I couldn't understand it then, because no experience of mine related to his. That I had given him little encouragement, little help through the years to mature spiritually, was becoming painfully clear. How could I though? I hadn't even been born spiritually then.

Jim had done the best he could. He took the children to Sunday school and church at the Nassau Bay Baptist Church, but with all the discord in our home, there was little more he could do. I had noticed that during the last few months he had been more involved in church-related activities—he had even shared his testimony before the whole congregation at his church and at another church in Houston. But we couldn't seem to discuss these matters. Once the lines of communication on a deep level are torn down, it is next to impossible to rebuild them.

So I earnestly prayed that first night that Jim's lunar adventure would be a powerful spiritual motivation and the beginning of a new life together. I also prayed that the Lord would not give Jim a minute's rest until he had completely surrendered his life to Him. When I finished, my heart was quiet and at peace, and sleep came easily. I had the assurance that God had heard my prayer.

Some months before the flight I had finally worked up enough courage to tell Jim about my conversion experience and that I felt I had really come to grips with my inner problem which had been largely spiritual. I knew I had to tell him sooner or later, but I preferred it to be later. He couldn't help but suspect that something was going on, for suddenly I had returned with renewed fervor to my church and had thrown myself vigorously into volunteer activities. In a sense, my church became my security blanket. This displeased Jim, as it always had, for he seemed to hate my church, the people in it, and all it stood for. If my pastor ever came to visit, Jim was rude and walked out of the room or went outside so he didn't have to be involved in conversation. Once when I brought my youth group home to make posters for their youth room, he wouldn't speak to them. The kids had expressed a keen desire to talk to an astronaut and ask questions, so I was embarrassed and hurt beyond description at Jim's behavior.

It was no wonder that I dreaded telling Jim. I knew he would either be intensely angry or give me the silent treatment—either response meant more rejection to me. I was right. He did become angry and misinterpreted everything I said and took it as a deliberate attempt on my part to displease him. The vegetarianism and no cosmetics aspect of my church's teachings annoyed Jim considerably, along with the Saturday observance which represented the inviolable Sabbath-keeping commandment to me. Although telling Jim brought on another conflict, our relationship was improving steadily as I learned more about depending daily upon the Lord's strength instead of mine.

For a few weeks after his flight, Jim worked incessantly on debriefing reports—first in our enclosed patio, spending hours writing, writing, writing, and later in his office where he registered his findings and impressions on a tape recorder. When well-wishers and friends became a constant interruption, he returned home to the patio. *Time* and *Life* magazines also had asked for written reports and personal observations from all three fellows, so although he was occupied most of the time, at last the children and I had our father/husband at home with us.

The year following the flight was so exceedingly busy that I had little time to reflect upon or assess any spiritual gains. It became necessary for me to relinquish all of my church activities and devote myself totally to traveling with Jim. NASA extracted a great deal of mileage from their astronauts, sending them all over the world as good will emissaries.

This time, I traveled *with* Jim whenever possible. NASA always included the wives and made provision for our accommodations and tours. Exciting, never-to-be forgotten adventures awaited us throughout the year, beginning with the ticker-tape parade in New York City on August 26, followed by dinner and a Broadway show with Mayor Lindsay and his wife.

Our itinerary for the year included a special "Jim Irwin Day" in Pittsburgh; an appearance in Washington D.C. where all three Apollo 15 astronauts addressed the joint session of congress and received a standing ovation; another ticker-tape parade in Chicago; a visit to the White House and dinner with the president and vice president of the United States; a lovely weekend at Camp David; a tour of Europe; an audience with Pope Paul at the Vatican in Rome; and a journey behind the iron curtain into Poland and Yugoslavia.

NASA controlled most of our time and arranged our travel, but our weekends were largely free. For the first time in years we could function as a family on these cherished days. Jim began to grow spiritually by leaps and bounds instead of the baby steps of previous years. I was growing along with him.

Almost every weekend Jim had an invitation to speak in a church or for some Christian group, so we usually packed the whole family into the car and shared the encounter together. What a thrill it was to hear my husband speaking openly to hundreds of people concerning his faith in Christ, especially when I remembered that he had *never* been able to communicate spiritually in previous years.

Then on October 27, 1971 Jim stood before 50,000 Southern Baptists at the Astrodome in Houston telling them of the spiritual impact he had received on the moon and how God had changed his life. After that appearance, word spread like lightning all over the country that Jim Irwin had a spiritual message he was willing to share, and the requests began pouring in.

Almost immediately Jim's pleasant weekend jaunts to meetings that had been mostly in Texas and accessible by driving mushroomed like an explosion, and we found ourselves flying all over the country from Florida to California, and from Chicago and Boston to New Orleans, and many points between.

Pressure began to mount as the invitations increased, so to save time, Jim usually rented a six-seat Cessna 320 and took all the family. Instead of just sharing his testimony, he began presenting the gospel in earnest and inviting people to accept Jesus Christ as personal Savior.

At NASA Jim had been assigned to the backup crew for Apollo 17, and every working minute for the next six months was supposed to be spent training for that flight. The routine of training for a third time, preparing to take the place of prime crewman Jack Schmidt, who undoubtedly would make the trip even if NASA had to wait for him if some mishap occurred (NASA was that intent on getting a scientist on the moon), held little interest for Jim.

It became more and more obvious that Jim's purpose for living was his increasing opportunity to share his Christian faith, *not* the NASA arranged public relations tours or Apollo 17. He did his best for NASA; however, a new excitement brightened his countenance as each Saturday approached.

Meanwhile, a dark cloud had been forming during that busy year of travel, and although I knew about the possibility of scandal, Jim kept much of it to himself. On the way home from Yugoslavia, flying high above the ocean, Jim leaned over and quietly spoke to me.

"Mary, I'm afraid we're in trouble over the envelopes."

"I'm not a bit surprised," was my matter-of-fact reply.

"I'm not either, I guess." Slowly and thoughtfully he chose his words. "The thing that disappoints me most is that I was unable to dissuade our entering into the envelope deal with the Germans. I

*The Moon Is Not Enough* 125

felt strongly that sooner or later the truth would come out, and our involvement would be revealed to everybody. But I was unsuccessful."

The whole envelope situation upset me so thoroughly that I refused to face it. I decided the members of the crew had gotten themselves into it, and they could get themselves out of it without any help from me. My mind was so closed that, to this day, I would not be able to explain what took place. However, Jim described it adequately in his book:

There was nothing mysterious about the problem we brought back from the moon—the envelopes. This was the most controversial development of the Apollo program, and, although most astronauts were involved to some degree, NASA made an example of the Apollo 15 flight. It all started with 400 unauthorized postal covers or envelopes that our crew took aboard. (We actually had about 650 envelopes in all, but more than 200 were listed in the manifest.) On our third day on the moon, we played post office and canceled the first stamps of a new issue commemorating United States achievement in space. With our own cancellation device—which worked in a vacuum—we imprinted August 2, 1971, which was the first day of issue.

The reprimand to our crew was the second ever issued by NASA. Curiously enough, the first went to Astronaut John Young for taking an unauthorized corned beef sandwich with him on the Gemini 3 mission, launched in 1965. As the spacecraft *Molly Brown* circled the earth, Young pulled out this hearty sandwich before the eyes of his startled buddy. I do not know whether John ate his sandwich or not. We certainly had to "eat" our envelopes.

I've said that of the 650 envelopes we had with us, 400 were not authorized. Of these, 100 were destined for an acquaintance in West Germany, Horst (Walter) Eiermann, formerly factory representative for space products, and known to the astronauts at Cape Kennedy. We split the remaining unauthorized envelopes, Dave, Al, and I each taking 100. I had never thought about selling mine; I hadn't decided what I would do with them, and we had no agreement with each other about them.

Walter Eiermann contacted Dave first, and then Al and I were brought in on the deal. The initial contact was back in May of 1971, and then we had two additional meetings with Walter. Our agreement was that the envelopes would not be sold until the Apollo program was over. It was our plan to use the $8,000 each that Dave and Al and I expected to set up a trust fund for the education of our children. This was to be in the distant

126

future, so the sales could in no way discredit the program. Dave carried the unauthorized 400 envelopes aboard the spacecraft in a pocket of his flight suit. The envelopes were onionskin and pressure-packed into a small and manageable parcel. We all three signed each one of the total 650 envelopes during the flight from Hawaii.

Dave mailed the 100 envelopes to Walter Eiermann in September, according to the agreement. We got a bankbook from Germany within a few weeks. Sometime in October, Dave came to me and said, "Jim, we are in trouble now—they are starting to sell the envelopes over there." We promptly sent back the bankbooks to Walter Eiermann, notifying him that he had broken the terms of the agreement and the agreement was off. We said that we didn't want to have anything to do with the deal. I don't know how Dave found out about the sale, but word had evidently leaked out in the European press. It was a tremendous blow to find out that we were being scuttled, actually torpedoed.[1]

By the spring of 1972, the envelope incident reached immense proportions and was being aired by the media. The amazing thing was that it took NASA eight months to learn that additional envelopes were being sold in Germany for $1,500 each. While the fuse on this powder keg was burning, all three men of the Apollo 15 crew were suffering, waiting for the explosion. Columnist Bob Considine wrote in July, 1972:

Shouldn't something be said in behalf of the Apollo 15 astronauts many of us seem to be righteously casting into exterior darkness for trying to set up trust funds for their children by selling philatelic "first covers" of their moon flight?

When they realized that they had made a mistake— though they had broken no laws—they cooperated fully with the prissy NASA investigation, turned over the major portion of the paperweight "contraband" to the authorities and expressed regret. But they were flown from Houston to Washington like criminals under extradition process, sternly reprimanded, and told directly or otherwise that they were no longer eligible to risk their lives for the U.S. space effort.

One would think that the space agency, with the lives of so many astronauts at stake, would show more compassion for its people. There must have been some gentler way of dealing with three fine men like Scott, Irwin and Worden. Why brand them for life, after offering actor and spacebuff Cary Grant the right to send anything of his choice to the moon in perpetuity? Why crucify these courageous pros who were paid less for flying to

[1]James B. Irwin with William A. Emerson, Jr., *To Rule The Night* (Philadelphia: A. J. Holman Co., 1973), pp. 227-228.

and from the moon than the union carpenter or electrician who
worked on their Cape Kennedy launch pad?

It's like arresting Marco Polo for double parking his gon-
dola after arriving home in Venice after 17 years at the court of
the Kublai Khan.

It was becoming obvious that Jim had lost interest in his job.
Even before the escalation of the envelope scandal, he and his
pastor, Bill Rittenhouse, realized that Jim had a vital spiritual message to share with the world. Although the ordeal of the scandal was
painful, for us it was God's instrument for the closing of one door and
the opening of another. It taught us clearly that nothing is wasted in
God's economy. Even our mistakes can fit into God's purposes and
bring glory to His name. It began to appear that God's will was for
Jim to go into full-time Christian work and for Bill Rittenhouse to
leave the pastorate and be associated with him. Jim distinctly remembered and related to me what we believe was the beginning of
God's call as he was riding down the streets of New York City during
his first ticker-tape parade with cheering crowds on either side: *You
are a servant to all the world now*, the message came.

As God's direction became clearer to Jim, he began to seek
advice from Christian leaders who would be in a position to guide
him in the formation of a Christian outreach program and recom-
mend initial procedure.

In June, 1972, Jim went to the Southern Baptist Convention in
Philadelphia and told the leaders of his denomination what God was
directing him to do. They offered to help us in every possible way,
and from the conversations with these Southern Baptist leaders
originated the idea that later developed into High Flight. The
objective was to create a nonprofit missionary foundation that could
support and direct Jim's efforts to share his message with people
everywhere. Bill Rittenhouse helped work out the design of the
corporation, and Jim named it High Flight after the title of the poem
by John Gillespie Magee, a young aviator who was killed in World
War II.

Astronaut Bill Pogue, Jim's close friend and source of spiritual
encouragement during Jim's pre-flight struggles, designed the High
Flight logo in the form of a vertical orbit representing man's reach
toward God, and a horizontal orbit representing man's reach toward
his brother. The orbital paths intersect in the form of the cross of
Christ, signifying the crucial nature of Christ in resolving man's two

greatest enigmas—his relationship with God and his relationship with his brother.

During Explo '72, Campus Crusade for Christ's spiritual explosion in Dallas that summer, Jim and Brother Bill Rittenhouse talked at length with Billy Graham sharing their dream and receiving valuable suggestions as to launching a new organization. Immediately after that, Jim and I sat by a private swimming pool in California and prepared a statement for the Baptist Press, and on July 30 the founding of High Flight was announced.

Jim's vision for the High Flight ministry was to share with people everywhere the inspiration he received from his space flight and his walk on another world and the renewal of his Christian faith resulting from that experience. The barriers that had always existed between science and Christianity could be resolved, Jim felt. And it was to these objectives that he sincerely committed himself before God and man.

When it became definite that Jim would take an early retirement and engage himself full-time in the ministry he had been cramming into every weekend, even before the development of the details of the High Flight organization, I began to dream of moving back into my beautiful home in Colorado Springs. I looked forward eagerly to redecorating, and in my mind already I had torn down the sun-worn drapes and replaced them with beautiful new ones, ripped up the old carpet and installed a heavy, bright shag, and walked from room to room deciding how I would change the decor. I could hardly wait to get started.

In the middle of the night early in June, however, just as I was falling asleep, God impressed upon me the fact that I must immediately detach myself from that home and the plans I was making. *You will never again live in that house,* a strong conviction swept over me. For a few moments I was crushed and couldn't understand. Then a sweet sense of comfort filled my bewildered heart as another message came. *I have something better for you, My child.* So I gave up my plans and surrendered our future to the God who plans all things perfectly. I realized we would have to "walk by faith" in our new life as never before, so it might as well begin. As it turned out, we would have another child—a circumstance I could not foresee—and the house would not have been large enough anyway.

In August we gathered our children and possessions and moved back to my beloved city, Colorado Springs, which was to be the headquarters of High Flight. Oh, the joy of returning to those "hills of home." I'd breathe clean, fresh air again. I'd see white, fluffy clouds against a deep, blue sky again. Every time I looked up, the majestic Rocky Mountain front range would inspire my soul. All the way "home" my heart sang out—*To God be the glory; great things He hath done!*

We left Houston with only a dream and the design of the infant High Flight Foundation. We had no money, no office space, no home, no staff except for Bill Rittenhouse and Louise Matthews, an unpaid volunteer for bookkeeping responsibilities. We had one important ingredient, though, in addition to the dream—*faith* that what God had begun in our hearts, He would perform. And that faith was sufficient to see us through the tempestuous first year.

The most exciting aspect of that first year came in the summer of 1973. Jim had been burdened for the Prisoner of War (POW) and Missing In Action (MIA) families, and Bill Rittenhouse had actually been a POW during World War II. As we started to pray for an opportunity to reach them, the idea began germinating for a summer retreat program in one of the beautiful Rocky Mountain ranches to which we would invite as many of these families to be our guests as would accept. A wealthy businessman in Houston offered to underwrite the cost of such a huge undertaking, so we pressed on with our arrangements of renting a ranch, engaging speakers, staff, counselors, and Christian entertainers. Invitations had been issued, of course, to the POW and MIA families.

Exactly one week before the opening of the first session, our Houston benefactor rescinded his generous offer, and we were left, so to speak, "holding the bag." Hundreds of plane reservations had been made and confirmed for families desperately needing and desiring the spiritual help we were offering. As our guests, we had naturally offered these families the week free of charge. We couldn't let them down.

Of course, we panicked when word came that there would be no funds. How could a new Christian organization like High Flight absorb so staggering a debt as faced us? Had we made our plans without the assurance that this was God's will?

The entire staff was driven to prayer and seeking the mind of the Lord before we even had the courage to open the retreat, and in the following five weeks we all learned in a new way to "walk by faith, not by sight." We literally "prayed down" the funds for the expenditures and necessities of each week. Many people loaned us large sums of money in addition to various gifts from others. Marvelous Christian celebrities like Anita Bryant, Norma Zimmer, and Andy Ferrier *gave* their time freely without charge, blessing everybody with their music and testimonies. Countless brokenhearted and bewildered war-shattered people were strengthened, and we saw couples reconciled who were on the verge of divorce. The priceless privilege of ministering to these people was worth many times the enormous debt we incurred and spent the next four years repaying.

And that is just how we view the unique ministry of High Flight. For the privilege of sharing Jesus Christ wherever God opens doors, Jim and I are eternally grateful.

### HIGH FLIGHT

Oh, I have slipped the surly bonds of earth
    And danced the skies on laughter-silvered wings.
Sunward I've climbed and joined the tumbling mirth
    Of sun-split clouds—and done a hundred things.

You have not dreamed—wheeled and soared and swung
    High in the sunlit silence. Hov'ring there,
I've chased the shouting wind along and flung
    My eager craft through footless halls of air.

Up, up the long, delirious, burning blue
    I've topped the windswept heights with easy grace
Where never lark or even eagle flew.
    And while with silent, lifting mind I've trod
The high untrespassed sanctity of space—
    I put out my hand and touched the face of God.

                    John Gillespie Magee, Jr.

# Object Lesson In Patience

As Jim landed the Lear jet he was learning to fly for his commercial license and began taxiing down the long runway toward the San Jose airport, we both were excited with the anticipation of meeting our new son. I had seen him briefly months before on a Far Eastern tour, but this would be Jim's first introduction to the little wide-eyed, olive-skinned wisp of a boy who would soon be calling him daddy.

Our search had begun months earlier after Jim and I had seriously discussed having another child. The only problem was that we *had* to have a boy. Jimmy was outnumbered by three sisters and desperately needed, we felt, another male in the household. His daddy had been gone most of his life, and the poor little fellow was so surrounded by females that we were seeing signs of "petticoat fever."

"I wouldn't mind having another baby, Jim," I finally conceded after exploring the subject, pros and cons, for several days, "but with my record, I'd probably produce another girl."

"Yeah, and that would be disastrous," Jim teased.

Deciding not to take the chance, we then began considering adoption. With four of our own children, we knew no American agency would even talk to us. We would have been laughed out of the office with so few children available for thousands of hopeful childless couples. So we turned our thoughts to the Orient since Jim's brother, Chuck, was married to a Japanese girl of whom we were exceedingly fond.

Scheduled for a Far East tour in October, 1972, we alerted missionaries in those areas to be looking for a little boy available for adoption. I really wanted a baby no more than six to eight months old, thinking there would be less emotional damage, hence fewer psychological problems with which to cope. But when I mentioned it, Jim was adamant about not wanting to be buried in diapers again, so I said no more. Secretly I was crushed and couldn't imagine why diapers would bother him, as seldom as he ever changed them. His thought, however, was to have fewer years between Jimmy and his new brother.

When we arrived in Japan and inquired, we were immediately told that the Japanese do not allow adoptions outside their own country. So we did not pursue the matter there, and our schedule was too demanding in Taipei and Hong Kong to allow time for visiting orphanages.

One free afternoon in Seoul, Korea, however, thirteen-year-old Joy and I took a taxi to a large children's state hospital. It was a wild, reckless drive speeding through the taxi-jammed streets of crowded Seoul, and I decided their driving philosophy was *never slow down—don't give an inch unless you're forced to*. I feared for our lives, but even more for the defenseless pedestrians vainly trying to cross streets. I concluded that the only way to get across a street in Seoul is to be born there.

We did arrive safely, much to my relief and surprise, and were taken to a ward filled with orphans. My heart ached as I walked from crib to crib gazing into each sad face, usually three or four children to a crib. Six-month-old babies often looked no more than six weeks.

One six-month-old baby boy named Tung, who appeared healthier than the rest of the children, caught my eye, so I kept that appealing little face tucked in the back of my mind while Joy and I scurried to the nearest department store for new baby blankets and diaper pins. At the hospital the blankets were so worn and faded, the diapers held together with small rubber bands tied in a half knot, that I resolved to contribute this small bit for the babies' comfort.

Later that evening after Jim had finished a speaking engagement and I had told him about Tung, we found a missionary to take us back to the hospital so Jim could see the little fellow. Even though the hospital was closed, a nurse kindly took us to the ward. Eagerly I clutched Jim by the arm and drew him to the crib, closely watching his face so I wouldn't miss his initial response. After all, bringing into your family a child who will vitally affect the household and every member in it is a momentous decision. We didn't want to make a mistake.

Strangely, Jim was expressionless. Then I looked down. The child was not Tung. Rushing over to the kind nurse, I demanded to know where Tung was. After much paper shuffling and questioning of various personnel, we sadly learned that Holt Adoption Agency had been in that afternoon and taken the healthiest babies to be flown to American adoptive families. Tung was among them.

Heartbroken, we left, knowing Tung was not God's child for us. We were learning a hard, but valuable lesson—discerning God's will through doors open and closed. Although the officials of that agency promised to send us a child when we got home, we both instinctively knew this was a closed door and that God was speaking to us through it. He was saying, "My child, when I close a door, it is for your good and My glory. Do not try to force open a way that is not *My* way. *You* cannot see beyond that door. I can. I have something better for you. Trust Me." It was hard, but I believed God, for I was learning to "walk by faith, and not by sight."

Our next stop was Saigon, Vietnam. Much to our surprise and delight, the missionaries there had done exactly what we asked. This had not been true in any other country. Three boys had been selected by three different missionaries for our consideration. Somehow I had an inner assurance that we would find our new son here in Vietnam.

This time I went alone. Jim had a speaking engagement, and Joy was playing with missionary children. My first stop was a Christian-sponsored orphanage toward the outskirts of Saigon. I was taken to meet little Cee who was eighteen months old and had strange-looking eyes that didn't focus properly. He was so malnourished that he was just learning to walk. Turning to the missionary, I shook my head and slowly said, "No, I don't believe this is the child for us, but thank you so much for your trouble."

My next appointment was with Jim Humphries, a director of the World Evangelism foundation. He had worked through another Christian organization, World Vision, and had located a little boy from the Sancta Maria Catholic Orphanage. When I finally found Chau Le Dong, he stood before me in a tan shirt, long white pants, and straw sandals, with his little chin tucked all the way down to his chest. Even when I spoke to him he would not look up. I knelt down to look into his face, but he would not lift his eyes, so I asked an

American girl standing nearby to take off his shirt to see if he had visible scars from the war. A prickly heat rash and a pink birthmark were all I saw on that tiny chest. Although extremely small for his three-and-a-half years, he was the healthiest looking child we had yet found. Something about him indicated that he had been loved. He never raised his head but kept toying with a small plastic butterfly in his hand. Just as I had known the others were wrong for us, I knew that little Chau, who had been nicknamed Joe at the orphanage, was right. I could hardly wait to tell Jim.

There was no time to see Joe again, but on the plane returning home Jim assured me he would trust my judgment and we could begin legal proceedings immediately. That Joe was almost four and nearer Jimmy's age greatly appealed to Jim.

It never occurred to us that adopting a Vietnamese child could be so complicated. We drove to Denver, a distance of sixty-nine miles from Colorado Springs, to pick up the necessary forms. In our ignorance, we anticipated two or three forms and a waiting period of perhaps a month since they knew in the Sancta Maria Orphanage we were adopting Joe. Five months, fifty notorized forms, and much confusion later, a phone call from Saigon informed us that Joe would arrive on March 5, 1973. How excited we all were. We could hardly sleep that night. And what a disappointment when the next day we received another Saigon call that Joe could not come until the United States and Vietnam settled a political problem. They would inform us when.

"Oh, Lord," I cried, "is this another closed door lesson? How can I bear it if we never receive this child who has lived in our hearts so long?"

God's Word came again, "For we walk by *faith*, and not by sight." So, after much agonizing before the Lord, I laid down *my* will, *my* desires, and could honestly say, "Lord, I desire Your perfect will above all else. I relinquish my longing for this child if it is not Your will."

A few days later a telegram came to tell us that Joe would arrive on October 11th at Travis Air Force Base in California. It was then we called my brother Paul, who lived in San Jose, and asked him to pick Joe up and meet us at the San Jose airport.

We loved Joe the moment we saw him. Our first glimpse was through the airport window. Paul, surrounded by his wife, Shirley, my mother, and Jim's mother and dad, was holding Joe and pointing to us. Joe could not understand Paul, of course, nor could Paul understand Joe's Vietnamese jabbering.

Before leaving Colorado, knowing his clothing would not be suitable for our cooler climate, I had purchased a heavy green jacket, relying on my memory for size. When I looked at the little fellow in his flimsy short-sleeved shirt, long cotton pants, and thin sweater, clutching all his earthly possessions in a small brown paper bag, I knew my guess was wrong and he would have to wait at least a year before wearing the new jacket. At least we could wrap it around him for now.

I took him in my arms, we greeted our parents and talked a few minutes, thanked Paul and Shirley, said good-by to everybody, then strapped ourselves into the waiting jet. We waved and Jim took off. No time wasted on this trip.

Joe sat on my lap as the plane lifted off the runway. Realizing he probably would be hungry, I had found a soup canteen at the airport, deposited a quarter, and brought along a cup of chicken noodle soup. He finished it to the last drop, then quickly fell asleep on my coat in the back seat. It had been a long, long trip for a little boy who hardly knew what was happening. He had been thrust from the only world he had ever known in his short life, however uncertain and unstable, into a strange, new, frightening one where nothing resembled the old and familiar. In addition to that, he had crossed the International Date Line flying to America, so it probably was the middle of the night by his little inner clock.

When we landed in Colorado Springs, Joey was awake and chattering like a magpie, pointing to every airplane he saw. Jim dropped the two of us off at a small private airport where my car was parked while he flew his plane back to Denver. I had promised the children I would bring their new brother by their school on the way home, and the stir he caused among the children probably disrupted classes for the rest of the day.

When at last Joe and I walked into our house, he began immediately inspecting its every nook and corner. He seemed to understand that he was home. That gave me time to look into the little paper sack he had held onto for dear life and only laid down as he became engrossed in other things.' His precious possessions amounted to a coloring book, crayons, a small rubber tractor, a pull toy, two pair of underwear, one shirt, one pair of pants—and an American flag. We never knew where the flag came from or whether he had the slightest idea of its significance. Also tucked into his bag were medical records and a chest x-ray from the orphanage.

I thought I had emptied it of all its contents, but later discovered the most precious item it contained. There at the bottom lay one of the sweetest letters I had ever read, written by a girl named Ann Marie who had loved and cared for Joey. She apparently worked at the orphanage, but when she knew Joe would be adopted, took him into her home for the five months of waiting. Her letter read:

> For the five months Chau was with us, he only brought joy and happiness into our life. We all love him very much. The house was so empty when he left. I hope he always remembers us. How is he now? He is a very lucky little boy. My brothers and sisters have been talking about Chau all the time. Does he speak English yet? I guess he can speak a couple words by now because he is a very smart little boy.
>
> I hope that he does not give you too much trouble. He is the only one alive in his whole family. I once talked to a lady who was at the orphanage when his mother first brought him. She was a fairly young mother and her husband was in the service and stationed very far away. She loved Chau and his brother very much, but she was too poor to raise them. She lived in the neighborhood of the orphanage and came to see them every day until the day she found out she was very sick. She died in a nearby hospital. His brother also died two months before Chau left for the United States.
>
> On behalf of my family and all the children at Sancta Maria, I would like to thank you for everything you've done for Chau. We will always remember you in our prayers.

The first time I ever saw our little lad in that Saigon orphanage, I had had the feeling he had been loved. The letter proved I was right. How thankful I was to have found this treasure, and how carefully I placed it with our most valuable documents so that when Joey was old enough to be troubled about his identity, he would have something tangible to help him know he had been precious to the parents who bore him in that faraway land.

In a few weeks we received a release paper from the Sancta Maria Orphanage identifying the child, his Vietnamese name, birth date, and verifying their agreement for his adoption. The last paragraph was expressive of the caring community he had come from:

> Mr. and Mrs. Irwin must pledge that they will consider little Chau as their legal child, give him an education and assure him a spiritual and material care. We agree to give Chau to Mr. and

Mrs. James Irwin for adoption so that he may have a bright future.

After outfitting him with new clothes and selecting a few toys, we settled down to the business of making Joe a part of our family. He loved the girls, especially Jill. Jimmy, however, was a great threat to him, so he kicked and punched him whenever he could. Fortunately, it was funny to Jimmy.

We learned never to take our eyes off Joe's hands or feet. He used his feet like another pair of hands, and if it wasn't a karate chop, then it was a karate kick he deftly administered to his unsuspecting victims. It became clear that swift movements, a hot temper, and tantrums had been his methods of survival in an orphanage full of aggressive children. He was not about to abandon these tried and true weapons, and because of the language barrier, for the first several months we could not penetrate his little mind to combat this hostile behavior. So we worked hard to teach him his new language.

Meanwhile, we had to endure the temper tantrums out of sheer inability to handle him. When a conflict arose and he began yelling and screaming, nothing in the world could stop him. The more we spanked or threatened, the angrier he became and the longer he screamed. The other children stood around in wide-eyed disbelief, as they had never been allowed the luxury of such unacceptable behavior. And I couldn't figure out what the problem was because I didn't understand the torrent of Vietnamese phrases. Gradually, as each day I patiently repeated words and phrases, our uncivilized karate expert settled down a little, and we began to communicate on a limited basis. Communication was painstakingly slow however.

The third week of little Joe's new life with us, just as he seemed to be feeling a bit more secure and was strongly identifying with me (he had begun that week to call me "Mommie-oh-ee"), Jim had his first heart attack. Our whole household was thrown into confusion. Jim was hospitalized in Denver, an hour and twenty minutes away, and I was forced to leave the children with a succession of ladies so I could be at Jim's side. At first Joe's whole world collapsed. He seemed fearful that I had abandoned him, and I couldn't blame the poor little fellow. That was all he had ever known. I made it a point to return every third day. Finally, after three weeks, the doctor said we could bring the children to see their daddy. When Joe walked into the room, he spoke his first English words. "Hi, daddy!" he said matter-of-factly.

As the months progressed, we observed unusual temperament traits, many of which we knew stemmed from his emotionally shattering experiences in war-torn Vietnam. Fear and hostility dominated his little mind and began expressing themselves regularly. He awakened often in the night screaming. Quickly I would run to his bed, pick him up, and hold him tightly until he quieted and dropped off again to sleep. For a long time these nightmares continued and even increased, and I was driven to the Lord. "Why, God, why must a child so small, almost a baby, suffer so?" Joey couldn't talk about it, of course, so we simply had to wait. Language was not the only barrier; his own emotions intervened even when he could express himself adequately.

Poor little Joey was a tragic product of war. His instinctive reactions, those he couldn't control for a long time, bore this out. One particular day he became angry with Jimmy over some trivial incident. He picked up Jimmy's BB gun, loaded it, and fired at a picture of Jimmy hanging on his bedroom wall. The next day I gave away the BB gun and was deeply impressed that it never would be safe to have weapons of any kind in our home. To this day, Joe is fascinated with guns and plays violent pretend games where everybody gets killed but himself. In his mind, I know he is still reliving the war, and I wonder sometimes if he will ever forget. After several years, however, he was finally able to tell me that in his bad dreams he still sees a soldier aiming a gun at him and awakens terrified.

As the temper tantrums continued and became even more intense, it seemed as though I could not find the key to helping him overcome these violent outbursts. Whenever I asked him to do something he didn't want to do—clean his room, pick up his toys, straighten his dresser drawers, come in from play—the only way he knew how to register his refusal was screaming, throwing himself down, kicking, and literally demanding his own way. I tried everything—splashing cold water on his face and over his head, spanking, threatening, loving, sitting him alone. Nothing worked. As a last resort, I tried walking away from him, closing his bedroom door, turning the radio up loudly, and totally ignoring him. Before leaving his room, I always told him, "When you finish crying, you may come out." Sometimes it would take an hour or so. The more he was allowed to express his anger and let it run its course, the more out of control he became. I had never seen such hostility, and began to fear that if this could not be checked, he would become a violent teen-ager or even a criminal. He had the perfect combination— deep-rooted anger coupled with a trigger-quick temper and a brilliant mind.

So frightened was I, that I called a psychiatrist friend, explained the problem, and asked for help. The doctor made a luncheon appointment with Joe and me so it would be casual, removed from the examining room atmosphere, and, perhaps, set him at ease. We discussed the problem openly. Afterwards when the doctor and I were alone, he told me to try the Z therapy, which amounted to three people holding Joe's entire body from head to toe so that he would be totally immobile. It worked beautifully for awhile. Then it occurred to Joe that he could have the undivided attention of three people and manipulate them at will, so we had to stop the Z method.

At last I went to the Lord and began my faithless plea with, "Why, Lord? Oh, why did You send me a child like this? I didn't need another problem. I already have two. What I need is a tranquil, easy child to enjoy." The heavens were silent. As I continued in this hopeless vein, getting no answers and receiving no assurance, I suddenly remembered something I recently had read in the Bible. "If you want to know what God wants you to do, ask Him, and He will gladly tell you, for He is always ready to give a bountiful supply of wisdom to all who ask Him."

Then I began to ask God what Joe's problem was and how I could help him. The answer was swift and clear. "I sent this child to you to *love*. That's all he needs—*love*." At first I thought God must be confused. He had another child in mind, for Joe's problems were too complex for so simplistic an approach. Surely he needed more than love. But the instruction came again. "LOVE HIM."

At this point, I wasn't sure I could. By now Joe had completely disrupted our household and had caused problems we had never before encountered. To make matters even worse, if Joe couldn't get to me in any other way when he was angry, he would turn and look at me with all the scorn he could summon and say, "You're not my real mother anyway."

Now that I had the key to unlock this little rebellious heart, I wasn't sure I'd be able to use it. How helpless I was beginning to feel. Again I prayed. This time it was, "Lord, I can't love Joe. And I see now that I can't help him if I don't love him. Please, Lord, would You love him for me? If You don't, it's hopeless."

As I recognized my total inadequacy and looked wholly to the Lord for ability to love this young rebel, a marvelous thing happened. My entire attitude toward Joey began to change. I could see that *he* was the helpless one, and only as the love of God poured through me could he respond and overcome the fear, anger, and hostility which were merely symptoms of the real problem— rejection.

The first breakthrough came one evening as the two boys were playing on the floor. Jimmy was on his hands and knees, and Joey was on his back with arms wrapped around Jimmy's neck. He leaned down in the midst of their laughter and whispered, "Jimmy, I love you." I was close enough to hear and to see the pleased grin on Jimmy's face and the twinkle in his eye.

When Joey was seven, he came to me and said he wanted to be baptized. I was startled, for he had never given any indication that he was concerned about his spiritual condition. So I asked him what he thought baptism meant. I wasn't surprised with his answer. He looked up at me with those black eyes and the most innocent expression and said, "It's when they dunk you in the water and everybody looks at you."

Obviously he wasn't ready, so I sat down with him and explained in simple, childlike terms: "Joey, when we are baptized, we are just telling everybody what has already happened in our hearts. You remember that we talked about sin in our lives and what it is. When we ask Jesus to come into our hearts and to forgive us and wash away our sins, then we have a clean heart and can begin to live for Him. After we do that, we are baptized so everybody knows our heart is clean and Jesus lives inside. Can you understand that, Joe?"

"Uh huh," came his noncommittal reply.

"Whenever you are ready to ask Jesus into your heart," I assured him, "Daddy and I will pray with you. Just come and tell me."

"Okay," he said as he slid off the sofa and ran to play.

It was a rather quiet, pensive boy who went to bed that night. With five active children, the incident was soon forgotten—we thought. Three weeks later, however, he came to me in the kitchen one afternoon and simply announced, "I'm ready, mom."

*The Moon Is Not Enough*  141

Bewildered, I looked down at him and asked, "Ready for what, son?"

"Ready to ask Jesus into my heart," came the solemn reply.

That evening Jim, Joe, and I knelt down and asked Jesus to fill our little boy's heart and make him the boy God created him to be. There was no doubt about his sincerity. It was beautiful to watch the transformation as Joe became more obedient and less rebellious. His emotional problems subsided, and the temper tantrums disappeared in a relatively short time. Two Sundays after this heartwarming experience, Joe was baptized. We knew he was ready.

Soon after Joe's conversion, he came to grips with the tragic loss of his entire family in Vietnam. It was necessary for him to relive that loss. First he saw his father, then his brother and mother. Strangely, he always saw his father as a single object, but his brother and mother as one. He wondered if he would ever see them again in heaven.

Trying to help him see that dying is a part of living, I told him that animals die and flowers die. He remained silent for several minutes, then sadly observed, "But the flowers came back in spring, and my family didn't." I drew him to me and kissed him and said, "Joey, there are *some* things we can never understand. These are the things we leave with God and simply trust Him."

Joey is eight years old now and has just finished the first grade. We held him back a year in the beginning, for he was not ready emotionally, physically, or mentally to start school. We have discovered through testing that he is a MBD child (minimal brain disfunction), apparently resulting from birth injuries, but that he can be helped through the special class he attends for children with learning disabilities. Joe is a gifted child, and we are trusting God to help him achieve his full potential.

We often remember the last line of the agreement we signed on the release paper, "So that he may have a bright future." That is our prayer for Joey.

# Taming of the Wild One

Joy, our oldest child, always reminded me of a tiny wild bunny we once caught. The little thing had found its way into my vegetable garden and was making havoc among the tender plants. For three weeks I tried to catch the hungry little vagabond but never could uncover its hiding place. Then while quietly weeding one day, I glanced over to the rhubarb patch, and there it was resting unsuspectingly under a huge leaf. I crept over, slowly reached out and scooped up both bunny and leaf.

The poor little thing, no larger than my palm, was frightened to death, and his heart thumped wildly against my hand. So I took him into the house and placed him gently in a large pasteboard box. Immediately he cowered in a corner. Later that evening I checked on him again, and he hadn't moved from the corner. Knowing that wild animals can die of fright, I slipped him into my bathrobe pocket so he could feel the warmth and closeness of my body. In a short time he relaxed and fell asleep. Before bedtime, I was able to feed him a little warm milk formula from an eyedropper.

At first, we had to catch him to feed him. Soon, however, he stood full length on his little hind legs and begged for milk from the toy bottle we borrowed from Jan's doll. Little Benjamin, the name we later gave him, became so tame that the children grieved when I told them it was time to release him and return him to the freedom wild creatures need to survive. I waited, of course, until the garden had been harvested.

Looking back over the years of Joy's life, I realize she was struggling against overwhelming odds which she didn't know how to handle and, consequently, spent her time, like the little bunny, running and hiding. Most of the months I carried her, I was in turmoil. If there is any credence to the current philosophy that the prenatal state of the mother's emotions deeply affects an unborn child, Joy couldn't help but pick up negative vibrations. By the time she was born, she was greatly desired, deeply loved, and showered with attention. Very early, however, she rejected that love and attention. Before she was nine months old, she did not want to be held, rocked, or cuddled; she would stiffen her little body and fight to get away. She was not like other babies, and I felt rejected by her and deeply hurt.

From the time she walked, Joy was a discipline problem. She tore up plants and magazines and got into everything. My lipstick, nail polish, face powder, kitchen cleaning compounds, anything she could lay her hands on, she smeared all over herself, the walls, floors, and furniture. I wanted desperately to enjoy her, but I found myself constantly correcting, punishing, threatening, coaxing, watching, fearing. There was no relaxing except when she was asleep.

During the first year of Joy's life, I was struggling to stabilize a new relationship with a husband of only a few months. It didn't help matters that Jill arrived when Joy was only fifteen months old. When Jill was two weeks old a hint of the source of Joy's problems should have been evident to me. Joy had never sucked her thumb, but she began at that point and continued until she was fifteen years old.

With two more babies born in rapid succession, it is understandable that I was too busy to analyze Joy's mounting problems. Rather, she simply got lost in the shuffle and had to find her own little world almost from the beginning.

By the time she was four, even though I was incredibly occupied with three little ones and expecting a fourth, I couldn't be oblivious to the intensifying trouble signals evident in Joy's behavior. She was taking things from the neighbor children and lying about it. Rather than looking for the psychological implications and handling the problem accordingly, I swiftly administered corporal punishment and probably left Joy feeling all the more rejected. With all my heart I wanted to be a good mother—a good wife, too. So often, though, I felt torn as to where my duty lay—in five different directions.

Joy was intelligent, but she used her keen mind, even as a tiny child, to deceive and to do what she *wanted* to do, not what she was *told* to do. She seemed to take particular pleasure in disobedience, with no apparent reason for her actions except that they had been forbidden. Jill's delight was to please me—Joy's to displease.

Although Joy had learning problems from the time she started school, they increased so much when we moved to Houston that we were advised to have her repeat second grade. I attributed these problems to moving, the new school, not knowing any of the children, and lack of concentration on her part. The latter reason became extremely apparent and frustrating when I attempted to help her with memorization. She couldn't sit still and couldn't repeat ten words without confusing them every time. My patience wore thin, Joy ended up in tears, and we accomplished nothing except more failure added to a growing list of previous failures.

By the fourth grade, along with her thumb sucking, rebellious spirit, and inability to learn, a new problem arose. She put on extra weight. My pride in my firstborn had already been severely damaged, and now I had to cope with a fat child.

Early in the fifth grade her teacher called to say that Joy couldn't sit still more than ten or fifteen minutes and, as a result, hardly ever received a complete explanation of her assignments. I was convinced that either she or I needed to see a psychiatrist. She was literally driving me crazy. I was already deep into marital problems, and my emotional state was deteriorating rapidly.

One day while having breakfast with Barbara Gordon and discussing our children, she suddenly inquired, "Mary, have you ever heard of dyslexia?"

"No," I quickly confessed, then laughingly asked, "What in the world is it? Some incurable disease?"

"Not at all," she assured me seriously. "In fact, four of my six children have had learning disabilities due to dyslexia."

Children with learning disabilities? Now *I* became serious and began to listen intently. The more we talked, the more Barbara's description of dyslexia sounded like my troubled child. For the first time, I was able to share honestly with someone the humiliating problems I had endured with this impossible child and my frustration at having completely failed as a mother. Barbara was extremely sympathetic, and as soon as we returned home she brought me her book on dyslexic children.

As I read the column of clinically proven symptoms, I began to cry. Joy was not deliberately impossible, and I was not crazy. This child had a medical problem and, best of all, there was help for her.

After I finished the book, I then found a doctor to prescribe the suggested medication to settle her down and enable her to sit still and learn. Hyperactivity was just coming under scrutiny and into public attention, so we at least knew the term. Except for a few initial side effects, the doctor's prescription helped.

Then I began to take Joy to a succession of doctors until at last I found a lovely Chinese research specialist, Dora Chau. Her specialty was children, so she checked Joy over thoroughly physically, emotionally, and mentally with a variety of tests. When the results were complete, Dr. Chau sat down with Jim and me, drew pictures of the brain so we could see exactly what the problem was, and explained thoroughly how Joy could be treated. Now I could have more compassion, but after ten years of harbored hostility and anger, I couldn't reverse my patterns of response. Perhaps if she'd been an only child and I could have spent more time both with her and studying behavioral psychology, I might have scored better on the motherhood scale. We did enroll her in a special class, and that year she brought home her first report card A. What a milestone that was!

During the summer of 1972 when Jim retired from the Air Force and we moved back to Colorado Springs, Joy was thirteen and entering her first year of junior high school. She felt alone and fat and ugly. And, quite frankly, she was. The tiny seed of rebellion that had been planted in those early years of rejection was now springing forth in full bloom. Joy began to smoke that year in the eighth grade, although she concealed this from us for a time. She substituted cigarettes for the thumb she had sucked so long. She dressed like a slob, traveled with a wild and rebellious crowd, and flaunted everything we asked her not to do or to do. Both Jim and I disliked her intensely, and there was no question about the fact that Joy disliked herself. It was, indeed, her total lack of self-esteem that drove her to all lengths of unacceptable behavior trying to prove she was no different than anyone else. Perhaps it gave her the attention she had craved for so long. One thing was certain; she received plenty of attention at home. All negative.

Whenever I thought things couldn't get worse, they always did, and for the next two years I was driven to the Lord with the same desperation King Asa in the Bible expressed when he cried, "Lord, there is none beside Thee to help." Being a fairly new Christian, I still labored under the widespread delusion that since I had given my life to Jesus Christ and was seeking to live it for Him, everything ought to be going my way. With each new crisis, I began to suspect that perhaps I had overlooked some minor theological detail. At least, it was not working as I thought it should.

Ninth and tenth grades were disastrous. Joy took no pride in her person, her room always resembled a pigpen or worse, she made no attempt to conceal her smoking and drinking, and she was making failing grades and skipping school regularly. All I could see ahead for this child was utter ruin and deeper humiliation for me. I didn't know which I dreaded the most.

Joy had hurt me so often and so continually that I began to build a protective shell for insulation against further pain. I also threw myself into a senseless round of activities so I wouldn't have to think. Jim was traveling a great deal with High Flight, and although we were slowly tearing down the walls and building bridges, still I was feeling the weight of the whole world on my shoulders. And a strange thing was happening. I, who knew all about walls and their deadly power to wreck human relationships, who had been struggling for so long to destroy the one between Jim and me, began building another. My subconscious rationale was to shield myself from further hurt. The thing I always forget about those walls is that they not only shut out hurt, but also love and tenderness. What I craved the most, love *for* this child and *from* this child, I unwittingly blocked. And it was my own doing.

I still hang my head in shame when I remember Joy's tenth grade, the deplorable events and near tragedies, both physical and spiritual. The worst part of it was my own mishandling of almost every situation. What a pity that we are forced to stumble our inexperienced way through the most important circumstances of life—marriage and the rearing of our children. Oh, I prayed a lot. But my quick temper and fast tongue were in gear before God could check me and give me His wisdom. I was like the apostle Peter. He was a man of action, never wasting time thinking when he could be speaking. And if things weren't moving, Peter would move them by force if necessary. He would do *something* right or wrong. It really didn't matter to Peter as long as he was doing or saying something. Until God touched him, that is. Then he could say:

> Dear friends, don't be bewildered or surprised when you go
> through the fiery trials ahead, for this is no strange, unusual

thing that is going to happen to you. Instead, be really glad—
because these trials will make you partners with Christ in His
suffering, and afterwards you will have the wonderful joy of
sharing His glory in that coming day when it will be displayed
(1 Peter 4:12-13).

And in another place:

. . . learn to put aside your own desires so that you will
become patient and godly, gladly letting God have His way
with you (2 Peter 1:6).

That didn't sound like the old Peter. But then, it wasn't. It was
after Peter had suffered bitterly. And so, through all my trials with
Joy, God was teaching me that He wasn't finished with me yet. Nor
Joy.

It was a good thing I asked God for a promise from His Word to
sustain me through those dark days. Joy hated me, and I had to
honestly say I hated her, painful as that admission was. I agonized
before the Lord for something to cling to. God gave me an unlikely
promise—one I didn't fully understand:

And it shall come to pass in that day, that the light shall not
be clear, nor dark: But it shall be one day which shall be known
to the Lord, not day, nor night: but it shall come to pass that at
evening time it shall be light (Zech. 14:6-7).

I had no idea as to the prophetic implications of that Old
Testament passage. I only knew that God was saying to me that
nothing was clear right now, but that someday it would all be light. I
believed Him, and the darker it grew, the more I clung to the
promise of light someday.

We had a miserable summer with Joy in 1975. She was between
ninth and tenth grade and hit an all-time low shortly after school
started. We really wanted to send her away to a boarding school but
couldn't locate a suitable one. I was frustrated about that, but
looking back, it was simply another part of God's mysterious plan.
*When would I ever learn to trust Him and to know assuredly that
every circumstance was allowed by Him and, by the time it reached
me, was God's perfect will for me?* How slowly I seemed to learn,
and at what a distance I often followed my blessed Savior!

Since boarding school did not materialize, we decided counsel-
ing might help. We took her to one psychiatrist with disappointing
results. We didn't return. The tension became so great that the
entire household was affected. All of us were at each other from

morning until night. I wasn't sleeping at night as a result of the continual worry.

Then one evening it happened! Friends were visiting, and we had planned to take them and all the children to the Flying W Ranch for dinner and western entertainment. Joy refused to go. I said, "Very well, you may stay home—but you had better *stay home* and be here when I return."

"Don't worry," she insolently mocked. "I don't intend to go anyplace. Can't you ever trust me?"

I wanted to slap her arrogant little face, but restrained myself and said instead, "You just better stay here, that's all."

The moment we left, she called a friend, and the two of them walked to a local teen hangout where the kids freely drank, smoked pot, and got into whatever other mischief they could devise. Joy had been forbidden to be at this place and, legally, was under age anyway.

Fortunately or unfortunately (I've never been sure), we returned earlier than anticipated, and she was just coming home. When she walked into the door and I saw her, I knew the end had come for me. "Young lady, you start packing this very minute," I unhesitatingly ordered. "I've taken all I'm going to take. You can find someplace else to stay until you decide to obey me."

At first she thought I was joking, but I stood my ground emotionless. When she had a suitcase filled, I told her to leave and that she would be welcome to return only when she decided to abide by my rules. Later I learned she spent the night in a sleeping bag at the far end of our wooded acreage. When she returned from school the next day, all her things were waiting on the porch, and the door was locked. Her friend and accomplice in rebellion took her in.

Joy was gone almost three months. Only twice during that time did I talk to her, and then by phone. Things at home settled down, and my frayed nerves began to mend. I had reached the point where I felt there was no help for her, and, besides, I no longer wanted to try to help her or get along with her. I felt that the welfare of our other children was being sacrificed for one who insisted upon wrecking her own life at the expense of the whole family.

For her fifteenth birthday, November 26, I made her a lovely green velour bathrobe with white trim. When I called to tell her, she seemed far away and wasn't making much sense. Although I didn't know it at the time, she was on drugs. When I related the incident to Jim, he could no longer endure Joy's absence and finally sought the help of a county psychiatrist who arranged an appointment for just the two of them. For the second session, the doctor asked that I come with them.

When we drove to Joy's high school to pick her up, she didn't want to come. It would have been easy for me to say, "Forget it," but Jim was of no such mind. Down deep I knew I had overstepped my authority by ordering Joy to move out without consulting Jim in the first place, so I sat in the car and kept still. Jim told her if she didn't come willingly, he would pick her up bodily and put her in the car. I hoped it wouldn't come to that. Joy probably outweighed her dad at that point. Finally he pushed her in. Then she began to whimper like a little trapped animal all huddled up in a corner. Her irregular, labored breathing and nervousness bothered me. I knew something was drastically wrong.

"Joy, are you on drugs?" I asked her at length.

"That would make you happy, wouldn't it?" she snapped back at me.

When we arrived at the county building, Jim had to push her out of the car and up the steps into the office. She was still whimpering and trembling.

All during the session, Joy refused to cooperate and kept tapping her foot and looking either at the wall or the floor. When the psychiatrist told Jim that Joy had entirely too much freedom and that we must get her out of her friend's home immediately, Joy began to whimper again. Then he told us that her friend's mother had called him, and it was evident that we were being undermined and our authority over this minor child flaunted. At that, Joy bolted for the door and ran down the hall with the psychiatrist in hot pursuit. We didn't move. After about ten minutes they returned, and Joy finally admitted that she had taken a large amount of speed and had more in her possession. The doctor told us to get her checked into a hospital immediately.

Jim and I stayed with her until she was safely in bed, then returned home thoroughly spent both physically and emotionally. The ordeal had lasted nearly five hours.

In less than an hour, when we had just finished wearily consuming a bit of needed nourishment (it couldn't have been called dinner by any stretch of the imagination), the phone rang. I thought about not answering, but while the idea was slowly taking root, someone else did. It was Joy—a tearful, apprehensive, humbled Joy. She asked me to go down to the basement phone so nobody could hear.

"Mom," the almost broken voice falteringly pleaded.

I forgot that I didn't want to help her, that I hated her, that I was glad she was gone. My mother heart reached out to her.

"Yes, darling, yes, what is it?"

"Mom, I just wanted you to know why I took those drugs. I just want you to understand."

"Yes, tell me, Joy. I'd really like to know."

"Well, there's this guy I really like, and I thought he liked me too. Then he told me I was fat and he wouldn't date me because I looked so awful." She began to sob.

"Oh, Joy, I'm so sorry," I assured her.

"Then . . . then someone told me I could lose weight if I took drugs, so I took a whole bunch of 'em to lose it fast."

"Oh, poor Joy," I exclaimed. My heart ached for her.

"Mom, what I have to say next is really hard—and I know I'll cry."

"That's okay, honey. I'm liable to cry myself," I said.

"Mom, I want to come home, and I'd like to have my room back."

Again my heart went out to her, and I knew I loved this firstborn child of mine no matter what had transpired between us. She was still my child, bone of my bone, flesh of my flesh.

I decided, however, not to answer her with the wild exuberance I felt, but to keep check of my emotions instead. "That's fine with me, Joy, but you'll have to ask your dad." Jim was having such a struggle taking his rightful place as head of our home, and I was having a struggle letting him, so I resolved not to overstep his authority again.

When we hung up the phone, we both were so overjoyed we were almost in tears. I ran to our bedroom to read again the promise God had given me. There it was, just like He said. "At evening time it shall be light." It was evening when that first glimmer of light shone through—but it was only a glimmer, only a beginning. The light was weak, flickered often, almost went out a time or two, yet I clung to the promise through it all.

Christmastime came before we knew it. Joy had been home a month. We were trying to learn to trust her, but it was so hard after the years of deception she'd put us through. She kept pleading,

"Why don't you trust me? How can I ever prove myself if you don't trust me?" So we decided to try once again.

Jim and I had been invited to Fort Worth to attend a colorful Christmas pageant. Our friends, the Walshes, had been asking us for two years, but we never felt we could leave the children. This year we would go and let Joy prove her trustworthiness by keeping the children overnight. At fifteen she should be capable enough for a twenty-four hour test. We let her know that we were depending on her, and if she pleased us it would increase our confidence in her greatly.

After the pageant we went to bed, but I could not sleep. My spirit seemed troubled. I began to pray, "Oh, God, please protect our children by sending angels to watch over them and guide them." I chided myself for worrying when, undoubtedly, they were all fast asleep in bed. After thrashing around for another hour, finally I woke Jim and related my fears. "Well, let's call them so we'll know," he suggested.

Jill answered the phone and assured us everything was fine, but I slept fitfully until morning and time to catch our flight home. I took an earlier flight than Jim and returned about 11:00 A.M. As soon as I walked in the front door, I sensed something amiss, although the house was in order and the children were smiling and telling me everything had gone smoothly.

My first clue was when I walked into the kitchen and noticed that the floor had been cleaned with kitchen cleanser and was gritty. The children's answer to my query was flimsy and unconvincing. "Oh, we just spilled something." Walking into the living room, I observed that the carpet had been freshly vacuumed even though I had left everything thoroughly cleaned the day before. Finally I asked in a loud voice, "What in the world is going on here?"

They all looked at one another innocently, shrugged their shoulders in a noncommittal gesture, and said, "Nothing. We just wanted the house clean for you when you came back." With that, they all scattered to their bedrooms, and I sat down for a bite of lunch.

I was so bewildered. I had been a mother for fifteen years and could sense when things were suspicious. Again I prayed. "Oh, God, what's wrong in this house? There is an evil spirit here. Please show me."

At that moment six-year-old Joey came running into the pantry to get something. I stopped him and asked what had happened while I was gone. His little black eyes widened, he gulped hard, and then it was out. "Joy had some of her friends over," he blurted, then quickly turned and ran away. Now I had concrete evidence to work on. So I called Jill.

"I understand Joy had some friends over last night."

She took a deep breath, her eyes had that "caught" expression, and then she told me Joy had invited about a hundred kids and they had a wild drinking and drug party most of the night.

I ran to my bedroom, flung myself across the bed, and sobbed my heart out. "Oh, God," I cried, "every time I try to trust her, she plunges a knife in my back. How long do I have to go on like this?"

After awhile Joy came up and tiptoed into the bedroom. I was still tearful when finally she spoke. "Mom, I'm really sorry. I didn't mean to hurt you so."

"Joy, how could you do this to me when I was trusting you? Didn't you know I'd be upset and you'd be in trouble?" I angrily demanded of her.

"Yeah, I knew you'd be mad," she admitted, "but I figured you'd get over it eventually."

"Child," I scolded, "you better get on with reality and get out of your fantasy world."

"I can't. It's too painful," Joy replied.

"Don't tell *me* how painful it is. I already know. That's where I live—in reality. And you're right, it gets painful. It is right now." I concluded the conversation and walked out of the room.

When Jim came home and heard the disappointing story, he was angry enough to ground Joy for a whole month. She was not allowed to go anyplace except school.

That night I prayed a difficult prayer. "Lord, please tear down the barrier I've built between Joy and me," I asked. "I only meant to protect myself from more hurt, but you didn't build barriers to keep from getting hurt. So please tear this one down and build a bridge of love and understanding to this child you gave me. Like you're doing for Jim and me. Make me willing to suffer hurt and to love her just the same."

Late in the spring of 1976 a noticeable change was apparent in Joy. For one thing, she looked a little thinner. After observing her for a couple of weeks and wondering why she seemed happier and easier to get along with, I finally asked, "Joy, what's happened to you? You seem different lately, and I think you're losing weight."

"I am, mom—both happier and losing weight."

"How come?" I persisted. "What's causing it?"

"Well, mom, I'll tell you. I just got so sick and tired of being fat, and I've tried every way I know to lose weight. So one day when I was all alone up on the porch, I decided to pray to God and ask Him to help me. I was only going to ask to lose weight, but I ended up giving Him my life and asking Jesus into my heart."

I was so stunned for a few moments that I couldn't think of anything to say. Then she continued.

"Ever since I prayed that prayer, it's a funny thing. I started losing weight right away, and I haven't wanted drugs or liquor or anything. And you know what? I always thought my friends wouldn't accept me if I didn't do all those crummy things. But it hasn't made a bit of difference. I think they like me just for me."

I began to cry. "Oh, Joy, I'm so happy!"

When I regained a little composure, I asked, "Joy, have your friends noticed any difference? Have they said anything to you?"

"Oh, yeah. They couldn't help it. When they ask what's with me, I just tell 'em I'm high on life now. They laugh, but it's the truth, mom. I never thought I could be so happy."

That flickering glimmer of promised light now began to shine more brightly. Joy lost twenty pounds in a brief time and from the fat prison emerged a tall, willowy golden-girl beauty who amazed everybody.

Though we've had our ups and downs, our good times and bad, we've been climbing steadily ever since Joy's divine encounter that day on the porch. Her rebellious, deceitful heart was transformed in that encounter, but the working out of it into her life is a matter of growth. And growth does not take place overnight.

Just before school was out for the summer of 1977, Joy's high school counselor told her she had won a $300 scholarship for a three-week course with Outward Bound, an organization designed to teach self-reliance and build strong character. This was an honor, indeed. I had heard that when a person finishes an Outward Bound course, they know who they are, why they are here, where they are going, and possess the confidence to do anything they undertake. I prayed this would be true for Joy.

When she returned, I knew my prayers had been answered. She enthusiastically related the many wonderful victories God had

154

given her; but, best of all, He gave her a promise to claim for her whole life:

> Whatsoever is born of God overcometh the world: and this is the victory that overcometh the world, even our faith (1 John 5:4).

I now see a quiet, gentle-spirited girl who is almost a woman. The rebellion is gone. God gave back that child He let me bear nearly eighteen years ago, though we had to go to the bottom of the pit and back again to accomplish it.

Joy is a leader. There is no question about that. How beautiful it is to see her leading others onto the path she missed for so long.

What the future holds for Joy, nobody knows, but one thing is sure. Joy's feet are on the solid path that leads to glory. Undoubtedly she will make mistakes adjusting to the freedom of leaving home and learning to make decisions on her own. But we are not afraid for Joy's future, for we know that freedom in Jesus Christ does not mean she is free simply to do as she pleases. Instead, she is free to become what God created her to be.

> If the Son shall make you free, ye shall be free indeed (John 8:36).

It is to this freedom we commit our child, our firstborn, whom we believe is a special gift from God for a special purpose in life.


> Dear God in heaven, you've heard my cries.
> Oh, you must have,
> they've been so loud.
>
> The cries of hurts
> so deep within me that not only I
> suffer from them.
>
> The cries of happiness
> from things I've seen, done, or know.
> All of them have been from you.
>
> Dear God, please help me to be
> as understanding and attentive to others
> as you are to me.
>
> Dear God, I cannot perceive
> the depths of your love.
>
> *Written by Joy at Outward Bound.*

# Death of a Rebel

"If you don't straighten up, I'm going to kill you," I screamed at Joy, shaking her vigorously as I threatened her. The moment those words poured from my lips, I was so startled and frightened that I clapped my hand over my mouth, uttered a horrified cry, and ran to my bedroom sobbing. I had become so angry that I had utterly lost control of my emotions. *Could I really have killed my own child? Was murder actually lurking in my heart?*

I didn't know. I only knew I had to get alone to think and pray this thing through. Parents do murder their own offspring in fits of anger, and child abuse is a major killer and maimer of innocent, helpless children. But how could I, a Christian parent, one who was really struggling to be an exemplary wife and mother, possibly be guilty of such behavior?

The crisis wasn't even that earthshaking, perhaps even a fairly normal succession of events leading to my irrational outburst.

Eleven-year-old Jimmy was old enough to have a go-cart we decided. There were strict rules, of course. For instance, he was never allowed on the highway. With our large acreage just outside Colorado Springs and long private road leading to the main road, there was no reason ever to drive off our property. Also, Joey was *never* to drive it. Headstrong child that he was, he was still only six.

When I heard the motor start that summer morning as I was working in the kitchen, I assumed it was Jimmy and never bothered to glance out the large picture window. Soon I heard Jimmy screaming, "Stop, Joe, stop. You'll wreck my go-cart. *Stop!*" I got outside just in time to see Joey tearing down the dirt road with Jimmy hanging onto the back dragging his body on the ground to slow the vehicle. When Joe heard me screeching, he stopped. I didn't wait for an explanation. On the spot I jerked Joey out and spanked him soundly.

Still a little shaken that afternoon, I heard the motor crank up again, I was pretty sure Joe wouldn't attempt the same thing so soon, but decided I had better check it out anyway. Walking over to the sliding glass door that opens onto our large front deck, I saw two cars pulled up to our road and people standing and looking at something. I raced down our long drive and reached the highway breathless and just in time to see Joy and Jimmy speeding down the road. Joy had a baby-sitting job and hadn't wanted to walk, so Jimmy kindly obliged her in the troublesome vehicle.

Twice in one day was more than I could handle. As I ran toward them, I loosened the heavy, wide leather belt supporting my jeans and prepared to use it. First Jimmy. Then Joy. The longer I whipped her, the angrier I became until at length she started screaming, "You stop hitting me," and began hitting back. That did it. I could easily have strangled her in the heat of my temper, and I knew it. It didn't matter that others were watching. I lost all ability to think clearly.

Now I understood why perfectly sane individuals are motivated to kill, but I didn't have a clue as to how to curb this uncontrollable reaction. Or, more accurately, how to control the circumstances leading to it. I knew other people must be struggling with similar questions, and a flicker of desire began to burn in my soul to share my experiences by some means and help those strugglers along their way.

The drama behind a story is often as intriguing as the actual story. Without delving into some of the behind-the-scenes action, this chapter could not have been written, for it deals with deep-rooted crippling emotions of which I was totally unaware. The tremendous task of writing this book may well be worth just the healing processes set in motion at the onset of the undertaking. Indeed, that might be God's purpose for it all.

The psalmist wrote, "Cleanse thou me from secret faults." In dealing with secret sin, God has shown me there are three catagories:

1. Sin that is hidden to others, but known to me.
2. Sin that is hidden to me, but known to others.
3. Sin that is hidden to me and hidden to others.

For a long time I had been asking the Holy Spirit to turn His searchlight into the deep recesses of my heart and illuminate the dark areas of which I was not aware. I sensed conflict within and a touchy area I couldn't define. Something was wrong in my spirit, and it flared up in the most insignificant circumstances and for unexplainable reasons, wrecking relationships and putting me at odds with everybody. I became hostile, critical, and unyielding. Since I couldn't unravel the mystery, all I could do was pray and ask God to reveal the hidden source.

God does not force His light, His healing, His correction, or His life upon His children. I was learning that He allows perfect freedom of choice. I could continue spiritually limping through life, refusing to allow God to dig down to the bottom of my problem, or I could give Him my willingness to deal with me, however severe He deemed necessary. Since I didn't feel I could mature spiritually until my spirit was cleansed, I came to the place where I gave God permission to do whatever was needed in my life.

Then He began. His first tool was a book whose title and contents I cannot now remember except for one statement: *We must claim back the territory for Christ that we have given to Satan through sin.* When I read it, I was pierced to the core with conviction. I laid aside the book, got on my knees, and asked God to bring to my mind all the territory I had given Satan through past sins.

Shameful memories began flooding my consciousness, insignificant incidents that had laid buried for years, forgotten. I remembered stealing a package of gum as a child. Then another miserable scene flashed through my mind. I was a third grader and had been put into the principal's office to do an assignment. Instead of working, I began snooping through all the desk drawers and found three pennies, a large sum to an eight-year-old in those days; I slipped them into my pocket and later spent them. Now the scene shifted, and I saw a check for $3.00. I was fourteen years old, had a summer job of pulling carrots and onions on a farm, and the territory I gave Satan with that first stolen package of gum had expanded. Three could so easily be altered to read eight. This took a little more cunning, but I managed. Greed must be accompanied by deceit, and I was becoming an expert at both.

On and on it went. Little incidents, long forgotten, flashed upon the screen of my mind with a freshness and clarity as if they were happening all over again. As the Holy Spirit's conviction bore down upon me, I reached for a pencil and pad to record all that God was showing me. Not only did I confess, having already laid hold of God's promise, "If we confess our sins, He is faithful and just to forgive us our sins and to cleanse us from all unrighteousness" (1 John 1:9), but I knew that if I was to claim back this territory from Satan, more had to be done. It's called *restitution*.

For the next several days I was busy tracking down names and changed addresses, making phone calls, writing letters, and arranging personal encounters. It was painful, mortifying at first, but each new confrontation worked such cleansing, such freedom into my burdened spirit that it became an exciting adventure. People were more forgiving and less judgmental than I expected. From some, particularly letters I wrote, I never received a reply. I had to rest these in the all-powerful hand of God knowing I had done all I could.

When I finished, though much cleansing had occurred, my spirit still was not completely free. So I returned to the Lord. The clutter of debris was gone, and it was not laborious to get at the heart of the matter. I simply asked God to put His finger on the remaining sore so that I might deal with it. Imagine my surprise when Edna walked right into my memory and stood looking at me. Astrology! Of course it was astrology! Though I had drifted away from its satanic hold, I had never dealt with it and reclaimed that vast territory from Satan, its author, and given it back to God.

Prayerfully I examined the whole astrology scene and my involvement in it. Why had I turned to astrology in the first place? Obviously, it was a substitute for God. I had known that for a long time. But I had never probed deep enough to understand that it was sin that drove me into it—the sin of wanting to control my own life instead of seeking God and letting Him have that control. It had been a heady experience to feel I could discern the future through astrology and govern my circumstances accordingly. So I confessed the wayward heart that drew me in the first place to occult involvement. Though I hadn't dabbled in it directly for several years, reading my horoscope was still a subtle temptation, and I had difficulty passing that page in the daily newspaper. Sometimes I didn't pass it. This I also confessed and asked God to deliver me wholly from any bondage, however slight, to this stronghold of the enemy. As I dealt with my sin, a clear realization swept over me that horoscope reading was the door Satan used in America to open the floodgate of occult darkness, witchcraft, Satan worship, and all their accompanying evils.

Then with horror it dawned upon me for the first time that my personal sin of astrology involvement was not nearly so great as that of influencing numbers of my friends to become participants, many of whom were still hopelessly entangled in its confusion. "Oh, dear God," I cried out when I thought of those troubled, searching souls I could have led to Christ, "how can I ever be free from this terrible responsibility?" I began to pray for them, one by one, as they came to mind. Suddenly, in the midst of the mental procession, my own children entered the picture. There they were. My innocent little ones for whom I had had astrological charts computed. And my husband. This was territory I had given to Satan and had to reclaim.

I searched my Bible for proof texts and positive support for this reclamation ordeal. God, who knows all about the hidden dangers of astrology, has issued many warnings, among them these:

> Don't act like the people who make horoscopes and try to read their fate and future in the stars! Don't be frightened by predictions such as theirs, for it is all a pack of lies. Their ways are futile and foolish (Jer. 10:2-3 LB).

> You have advisors by the ton—your astrologers and stargazers, who try to tell you what the future holds. But they are as useless as dried grass burning in the fire. They cannot even deliver themselves! You'll get no help from them at all. Theirs is no fire to sit beside to make you warm (Isa. 47:13-14 LB).

> So why are you trying to find out the future by consulting witches and mediums? Don't listen to their whisperings and mutterings. Can the living find out the future from the dead? Why not ask your God? . . . I have not sent them, for they have no light or truth in them (Isa. 8:19-20 LB).

How could I ever have imagined help could come to me from so uncertain a source? If I had been seeking in the right place, I would have known the folly of it.

Finally I found the instruction in God's Word which I needed to tear down this enemy's stronghold;

> For the weapons of our warfare are not carnal, but mighty through God to the pulling down of strongholds; casting down imaginations and every high thing that exalteth itself against the knowledge of God, and bringing into captivity every thought to the obedience of Christ (2 Cor. 10:4-5).

When I finished taking authority over Satan and handing back to God all the ground I had lost, I knew this facet of the internal cleansing I needed was complete. Then I gathered all the children and told them what I had done, particularly where they were concerned in the astrology part.

Just before Easter on April 4, 1973, when it seemed we were getting things all together and making more progress toward family unity, I received a shattering phone call. We had just signed final papers for our new little son, Joe. Joy, although always difficult, had not yet entered the rebellion that almost destroyed us; and the only major problem Jim and I seemed to have at this point was his constant traveling for High Flight and consequent neglect of the family.

It had been a trying day anyway—one of those days when everything goes wrong, and the first mistake I made was getting out of bed that morning. At 4:30 P.M. I had just returned from a Brownie Scout meeting where I had "lost my cool" and confronted the leader with her unfairness to some of the girls, my Jan included. I left unnerved and arrived home in the same state. When the phone rang and the voice at the other end identified itself as a doctor, informing me that my husband had suffered a heart attack, I thought the call might be some prankster, as I had been reading in the newspaper of similar cruel practices in the area. Immediately I blurted, "Is this some kind of crank call? I don't think it's very funny."

The poor doctor must have thought he had gotten hold of a half-wit as he patiently reiterated that he was, indeed, a doctor, and that Jim had really suffered a heart attack, and that he thought I should get myself to Denver immediately. I apologized profusely, hung up the phone, and burst into the tears I had suppressed several times during the day.

When the children heard me, they rushed to my side alarmed. "What's the matter, mother? What happened?" At last I stopped sobbing enough to say, "Your father is in the hospital in Denver. He just had a heart attack." Then *they* began. We all cried together for twenty minutes or so, then I got hold of myself enough to quiet the children and suggest we have a time of prayer before I left. After hastily calling for a sitter, I drove the sixty miles in a state of complete shock, praying as I went. All I could think in my distraught condition was that now, after all we had been through to get our home and lives in order, I would lose Jim. He had been close to death so many times and always pulled through. *Oh, dear God, surely You're not going to take Jim now. We've been through so much, and we're just now learning to live together.* "Please let him live—oh, please let him live!" I cried over and over again.

With no assurance that he *would* live, I saw him briefly. There were tubes in his mouth and nose, needles in his arms, legs, and feet, and complicated-looking machines all around him. He had been sedated, and though he recognized me and spoke, his mind was hazy and his expression blank. Walking out of that dismal room, I wondered if I would see him alive next time.

Arrangements had been made for me to stay in the guest room at Fitzsimons Hospital. As I lay there alone that night, I thought and prayed. Again I sifted through the tangled events of our life, beginning with that first moment when I had looked up into Jim's face in the photography shop. In some ways it seemed like a hundred years ago—in others, just yesterday.

At length I knew I must commit Jim totally to God and somehow find rest for my anxious heart. Promises from the Bible began slowly to seep into my mind.

"All things work together for good to them that love God" (Rom. 8:28). *Do I love You, God? Enough to claim this promise? Yes, I do. God, You know I do.*

"In everything give thanks" (1 Thess. 5:18). *Oh, but that's so hard right now. How can I thank You for this disaster? Surely You don't expect it from me when my whole future is being destroyed. I don't feel thankful. Oh, God, how can I praise You when Jim's life might be slipping away this very hour?*

I wrestled with this one for some time. Then I repeated it again aloud: "In *everything* give thanks, for this is the will of God in Christ Jesus concerning you." As I said it, I saw it as never before. God did not say *if you feel like it,* or *if circumstances warrant it.* What He really said was in *everything*—in every circumstance, good or bad, whether you feel like it or not—give thanks. I saw it as a firm command, not a matter of choice. If I was to be obedient in this crucial moment, I must thank God for this tragedy whether or not I understood it, whether or not I could see the outcome—"for we walk by faith, not by sight" (2 Cor. 5:7).

My first attempt was half-hearted, tongue-in-cheek, and before I even finished, "Father, I thank You for Jim's heart att . . . ," I

162

began sobbing uncontrollably. I pulled myself together and started over, determined to obey God if it killed me. And I thought it might. But to my astonishment I felt more sincere, and as I continued, the inner pain eased. Before long, my heart became joyous and full of anticipation. Faith rose, and soon I could believe that this thing *would* work for good in our lives. It was then that I saw it—as clearly as if it actually took place before my very eyes. I saw on the screen of my mind Jim's heart as he lay on that hospital bed. Instantly a large hand, God's hand, reached over and covered his heart. I knew God was telling me that Jim was safe in the hollow of His hand. Complete peace swept over me, and I fell asleep immediately.

Jim's recovery was slow but sure. God not only worked in me, but in Jim as well. Jim battled inwardly with the possibility of death and for the first time accepted human weakness and his need to be totally dependent upon the Lord. He rearranged his priorities as well.

When Jim had fully recovered and was back in his High Flight ministry of traveling and speaking around the world, it seemed that God was gently nudging me in the direction of writing a book. My first surprised reaction was, "A book? Who me? What do I have to say that anybody would be interested in reading?"

As the idea recurred, I shrugged it away wondering whatever in the world put it into my head in the first place. But it kept recurring, so I began to pray about it. At length, it became so insistent that I could ignore it no longer. For whatever reason God had in mind, I knew He was placing this urgent desire in my heart.

In the summer of 1975, the urge to tell my story was so compelling that I took two weeks from my busy home schedule and taped as much as I could remember. Then I sought the advice of acquaintances in the publishing world. It was always the same. *You obviously have a story to tell, but you must find a writer who could do it justice and write it in readable fashion.*

Though various writers were recommended, I had no peace about working with someone halfway across the country. Neither funds nor time were available. So I prayed, "Lord, it was Your idea in the first place for me to write this story. Now I've done all I can. I've been obedient. If You want it written, You'll have to find a writer and a publisher." With that prayer, I inwardly laid down the project and reached for my Bible. Matthew 7 was my Scripture portion for the day. I read, "Ask, and it shall be given you; seek, and ye shall find; knock, and it shall be opened unto you; for everyone that asks receives; and he that seeks finds; and to him that knocks it shall be opened" (Matt. 7:7-8). The moment I finished reading those words, the name Madalene Harris flashed into my mind. *Madalene Harris. Of course. Why didn't I think of her before?* She was only a casual acquaintance, but I knew she was a writer, and instantly I recognized this was God's answer. I was so sure of it that I forgot to call her for almost three weeks. When finally I got around to calling, I knew without the slightest doubt she would write the book. It took *her* several weeks to arrive at the same assurance, but soon I knew she was the only person in the world who could write my story as if it were her own because of parallel experiences. Before even receiving her answer, I rushed over to her my two weeks' labor that had been transcribed from tape to type.

The frantic Christmas holiday intervened before our next meeting. Early in January 1976 I called Madalene for an appointment to discuss the book. What transpired was not at all what I anticipated. I was ready for a glowing report, eagerness to tear into the exciting project, and gratefulness that I had asked her. Obviously, I did not know her well.

She looked me squarely in the eyes and said with great conviction: "Mary, *if* I were to write your book, it would be absolutely necessary for us to have a totally honest relationship. Neither of us could hide anything from the other. You would have to share with me things hidden from all eyes but God's. And I would have to be free to tell you exactly what I think whether you liked it or not. Are you ready for that?"

"Of course," I replied without a second thought.

She was silent for what seemed like several minutes. Then she picked up the ninety-eight typewritten pages I had previously given her, waved them toward me, and asked, "Do you want to know what came through to me from reading this manuscript?"

"Yes, tell me," I said eagerly.

"From start to finish, two things are plainly evident. A rebellious spirit and total lack of submission to your husband," was her shocking reply.

"But . . . but . . . I wrote a chapter on submission," I stammered.

164

"You can write or say anything, Mary. It's living it that counts. And you're not living it."

"But . . . but . . . I really feel I've dealt with that problem and have it squared away." I was on the defensive now and not too convincing.

"Just for starters, then, what's this business about *his* church and *my* church?" she demanded. "And what's all this complaining about Jim not letting you go your way religiously and leaving you alone in that area?"

"But I don't go to *my* church any more," I argued. "I go to *his.*"

"That may be true, Mary," she said thoughtfully. "But I have an idea you are like the little boy in the familiar story who kept standing up on his chair at the dinner table. Several times his mother sat him down. Finally, he looked up at her defiantly and said, 'I may be sitting down now, but in my heart, I'm still standing up.' In your heart, Mary, you're still standing up." It was to be more than a year before I fully understood the meaning of "still standing up" and recognized that Madalene Harris was right.

For the moment I was angry. Quickly I retorted, "Well, the Bible says that we ought to obey God rather than man, doesn't it?" I knew I had her there.

"Of course it does, if you want to pull it completely out of context. In the first place, that's not speaking of husbands. If it were, then it would clearly contradict other passages of Scripture."

"Tell me, Mary, about your children." She seemed to change the subject. "Are they doing well? Are you proud of them? Are they obedient?" Then I knew she hadn't changed the subject.

First I told her about Joy who was in complete rebellion and driving me almost insane. I cried as I spoke.

"How about the other children?" she probed.

"If I'm going to be honest, I'll have to say they're all in rebellion," I reluctantly admitted.

"I could have told you that, Mary. Do you know why?" she asked.

By now I suspected the answer, but I replied, "No, why?"

"Because their mother is in rebellion. As soon as you deal with it, they will also."

She did not give me an answer that day as to whether or not she would write the book. She merely said, "You *must* deal with your rebellious heart before I can consider writing your book."

I knew I was stubborn, but I had never seen it as rebellion, nor could I have admitted the truth had not the Holy Spirit prepared me for this revealing encounter. Here was *sin that is hidden to me, but known to others.* I had been praying for cleansing from secret sin. How would I react now that I was exposed?

As I drove home, I sincerely asked God to deal with my rebellious spirit, and by an act of my will, I gave God permission to get started with me and stay on my case until I was thoroughly cleansed. He made it clear that I must tell Jim, admitting how wrong I had been. Though this was a tremendous blow to my pride, I so desperately longed to get my life and my family straightened out and to walk in obedience to God that I was ready to do anything.

After relating to Jim the rather humiliating encounter I'd just experienced, before giving myself an opportunity to change my mind, I plunged into an apology.

"Jim," I cautiously began, "I didn't realize my spirit was so rebellious and unsubmissive, and I want to tell you I'm sorry I have not allowed you to be the head of our home. I may not always agree with you, but I'm going to try to let you make all the decisions in the future."

I expected him to throw his arms around me, congratulate me, and tell me I really hadn't been so difficult after all. Instead, his terse comment caught me off guard. "Well, I *will* have to admit that you've really made it rough on me."

I swallowed hard, trying not to retaliate with an angered defense and counter accusation.

In a moment he continued, "If that's the case, I'd like to ask you *never* to attend your church again. I don't see how we can ever be a family unit if the two of us are constantly moving in different directions."

Although I tearfully agreed to his request, I didn't feel at all emotionally ready to take this step. I felt like a little child whose thumb and blanket had been torn away from him. Indeed, that is exactly what took place. I didn't understand at the time, but my obedience enabled me a year-and-a-half later to see clearly that my church had been my security blanket; God had to literally "yank" it away so that I could grow up spiritually and learn that church and denomination are not the basis of my security. Jesus Christ alone is sufficient.

Thinking about the conversation with Madalene, my rebellious

166

children, and now the root of the whole dilemma, something in the Bible came to mind that I'd never quite understood. It had always seemed unfair, so unlike a loving God of grace and mercy. Now it was becoming clearer. It said: "The sins of the fathers will be visited upon the children" (Exod. 20:5). I had always supposed this meant that if I committed a sin, my children would pay for it. "Why," I asked myself, "should innocent children suffer when they were not to blame?" In essence, what Madalene was saying was, *You are in rebellion, and because your children look up to you as a model, they are imitating your character traits; therefore, they are in rebellion.* My sin *was* being visited upon my children, and she was right. If I didn't deal with it, neither would they. What an awesome responsibility. Here was more territory I had given to Satan which I needed to reclaim for Christ.

# Freedom at Last

"Unto the third and fourth generation," the Bible warned that the sins of the fathers would be visited upon the children. *Where am I in this chain of rebellion generation-wise*, I wondered. I knew I must talk to my mother, so I prayed I would have the opportunity soon.

Two weeks later I found myself sitting in Oregon across from my mother. An unexpected trip to the West Coast had evolved, and Jim agreed to take me along and let me have a day with my aging parents. My mother sat in her favorite rocking chair as I began.

"Mother, God has really begun to work in my heart and to reveal some ugly things I must deal with. I never realized that one of my main problems is rebellion, but I can't get to the bottom of it unless you tell me how I got this way. What makes me so defiant and determined not to submit to authority? If someone tells me I can't do something, I move heaven and earth to prove I can and will. I've always wanted my own selfish, stubborn way, and it seems I'm forever trying to keep people from taking advantage of me and to prove that I'm better than anybody else."

After a little probing, mother began telling me a story I had never heard—how my grandfather had migrated from Norka, Russia, finally arriving in America by boat with his young wife, mother-in-law, and a few other family members. They settled in Oregon, homesteaded a small parcel of land, and began farming. He longed for sons to help him on the farm. His first three children were daughters, and his wife died giving birth to their fourth child—the longed-for son, who also died. In a very short time he remarried, and the next child born was my mother. Another sister came along shortly after that. Then there were no more children.

168

My grandfather, it seems, was bitter at the loss of his only son, and during the months before my mother's birth, he stubbornly set his will that this child would be a boy. At her birth, he was so disillusioned and embittered that he hated this girl child and determined to vent his wrath upon the object of his disappointment. He blamed God and never forgave Him, taking out his vengeance upon my mother and beating her with little provocation. The seeds of hatred and rebellion sprang up in my mother's heart, and she married at an extremely early age to escape her father's mistreatment.

"I made up my mind, Mary, that it would be a cold day in hell before another man treated me like my father did," she told me with eyes flashing and chin quivering.

"Mother!" I exclaimed in shocked disbelief. "Then you've *never* forgiven your father for what he did to you. You still hate him, don't you?" What a revelation! I'd never viewed my parents as people. I'd never had an adult relationship with them nor thought of them as human beings with the same struggles, same temptations, same failures others experienced.

Instantly the whole picture came into focus. My mother, as good and wholesome a woman as ever walked the earth, had lived all her life with this bitter hatred seething within, poisoning her spirit, making her incapable of warmth and loving relationships, and, most tragic of all, producing a defiant rebellion in her spirit. It began with her father, transferred to her husband, blighted her children, and spread its infectious tentacles to all who surrounded her. I could begin to trace the development of this chain now and see that the source of rebellion is a wounded spirit; it progresses to rejection of authority and moves on to bitterness and ultimate self-destruction in one form or another.

It's true, mother was an innocent victim. But I saw more clearly than ever that we are absolutely responsible for *our* reaction to the sin of others against us. I cannot prevent people from sinning against me, but I can, with God's strength, prevent a retaliatory spirit in response to their sin. The Bible says, "Sin, when it is finished, brings forth death." A grim reminder of this truth was facing me.

As we talked, my mother realized she had never identified nor dealt with her bitter feelings. She had felt justified, placing all the blame where, according to all human reasoning, it belonged. As I unfolded to her God's plan for releasing us from the cruel bonds of bitterness and rebellion, she began to cry. Then we prayed together, and mother confessed her sin of hatred, asked God to heal her, and forgave her father for his years of angry mistreatment. My mother and I began a new relationship that day.

"This rebellion in our family is going to come to a screeching halt, beginning with me," I told the children upon my return home as I carefully explained my disobedience, where it had all started, and the steps to freedom. The children were quiet, introspective, and seemed to understand. Though we had a long way to go, this proved to be a healthy beginning, and all seven of us started to move toward family unity and harmony in a new way.

I knew we were ready now to start the book. I also knew that Madalene Harris would consent to write it. When I called her, she confirmed that God had been working in her heart and she was ready to begin. We both committed ourselves to whatever it would take—hard work, long hours, unforeseeable problems and obstacles. And we've had them all.

That same summer a cherished desire blossomed into reality. For two years I had been longing to attend the Clyde Narramore Clinic and Seminar. I had not known of this ministry until Teddy Heard, a special friend of mine (who went to be with the Lord that year) and wife of Houston's Judge Wyatt Heard, asked me, "Mary, have you ever heard of Clyde Narramore?"

Perhaps for pride's sake, I had not shared with Teddy or anyone the problems we had within our family and the communication breakdown between Jim and me, even though vastly improved over previous years. However, her statement, "Attending the seminar makes good marriages even better," planted that seed of desire, although I really never dreamed it would be possible. Five children? A husband with a pressured schedule? *Don't waste your energy, dear. Save it for the realm of reality.*

Suddenly, with almost no planning, I found myself going—and with Jim. We arranged care for the children, called the Narramore Clinic for reservations, and took off.

It seemed the entire first day or so all we did was psychological testing. The rest of the time was spent in conferences, but each person attending the seminar was allowed a free session with a trained psychologist to interpret the results of the tests. Wayne Colwell, my counselor, picked up the outstanding clue in all that battery of questions and answers: I had a serious identity problem.

    Question: Who are you?
    Answer:    Jim Irwin's wife.

There it was. I really didn't know who I was except as an extension of my husband. I did not see myself as a person in my own right. So Dr. Colwell began asking me to enumerate what I could accomplish on my own if my husband were to die. Much to my surprise, I was able to think of several things. He smiled. "See, you really know who you are. You just thought you didn't."

When I realized I was important to God just as Mary, and that I had many talents and abilities, I stopped feeling worthless and allowed my true identity to emerge. *I was not an extension of anyone. I was ME*, Mary Irwin, completely capable of achieving on my own and letting my failures produce growth instead of guilt and defeat. What a milestone!

My relationship with Jim immediately improved as I gained a stronger self-image and viewed myself as a worthwhile, important person. Out of this grew the courage to face a crippling emotion I hadn't dared contemplate—fear of rejection. It had begun first, of course, as a young child rejected by overbusy parents, and was reinforced by the older brother I adored going off to war, by Jim's demanding career necessitating absence from the home, by his near death from accident, heart attack, and open-heart surgery, and now by his constant traveling with High Flight. Deeper and deeper I had plunged into despair and self-pity as I interpreted all of these as rejection. My sense of worth plummeted as I nourished the "poor me—nobody loves me" syndrome. I had spent my life trying to gain acceptance by being what I thought other people wanted me to be, thus confusing myself, hiding behind a facade, and losing my identity in the process. Now that I was becoming *somebody* in my own eyes, I could come to grips with this most common of all fears— rejection—and the inner loneliness accompanying it.

When I saw it all clearly, I set my will to forgive everybody I thought had rejected me, beginning with my parents and ending with Jim. Then I laid down bitterness, resentment, and hatred. Finally, I fully accepted the fact that *God accepts me* just as I am. He doesn't just tolerate me—He loves me unconditionally.

As Madalene and I began to work on the book in earnest, we spent hours and days and weeks laying groundwork, sifting through every facet of every experience. It was easy to cite facts and happenings, but Madalene was never content with the superficial. She forced me to plumb the depths of my emotions, reactions, and to evaluate my hang-ups and fears. Most of the time I left our sessions wrung-out, drained—in popular terminology, a basket case.

During one of these heavy encounters, I realized for the first time that though I had asked God to forgive me for past sins and my before-marriage pregnancy, I had never *really* forgiven myself. Somehow I kept whipping myself for this and felt I wasn't as spiritual as other people. How could I be and have committed such a terrible sin?

But how do you forgive yourself? I wrestled with it for some time, then decided to ask a Christian friend.

"What you are saying, Mary, is this," she wisely told me. "'Jesus, what You did on Calvary wasn't enough. This sin is so bad, I must continue to punish myself over and over.'

"Do you know *how* you are punishing yourself, Mary?" she continued. "By withholding self-love and self-worth. You must accept God's total forgiveness and thank Him for the privilege of forgiving yourself."

"But I've tried to do that, and I always feel just the same—worthless," I confessed.

"In the first place, Mary, you cannot rely on *feelings*. They are never accurate. The *fact* is that God has totally forgiven you. It doesn't matter how you feel about it. Secondly, it's not a once-for-all transaction. On God's part it is, but we are so human that we take our eyes off God's provision and place them on our failures. So whenever you think about the mistake you made years ago, simply thank God for His perfect forgiveness and for the privilege of forgiving yourself."

As the writing of the book progressed, slowly and painstakingly because it wasn't always easy to remember the necessary details, we began to pray in earnest for the publisher of God's choice. Clearly we were led not to seek out a publisher in any way. *I will send you the right one at the right time* was the unmistakable instruction. After several months and in the most astounding fashion, we received a long-distance phone call from Grand Rapids, Michigan, for an appointment to discuss with an astute, internationally known publisher the possibility of a contract.

On the very day of the appointment, January 7, 1977, Jim had to undergo emergency open-heart surgery in Houston, so I had to fly out without being able to contact the publisher. Although it was a crushing disappointment to miss the engagement, I committed it to God and boarded my plane. Madalene kept the appointment with Robert DeVries, and by the time I returned, promise of a contract was assured.

Again I had to face the grim possibility of being a widow. This time, however, I was able to trust God implicitly—not just for Jim's life. At last I could say, "Lord, *whatever* Your will is for my life, I accept it with thanksgiving. If You choose to restore Jim's health, I praise Your name. If You choose to take him home with You, I still praise Your name."

Jim seemed to recover beautifully from the delicate by-pass heart surgery. He began to walk each day, lengthening his distance and setting new exercise goals regularly. Soon he was spending each morning in the High Flight office and beginning to resume his travel schedule. The doctor told him he could do anything he felt like doing.

That is not a safe thing to tell Jim Irwin. He has never known limitations, physical or otherwise, and at forty-seven years of age, it is hard to change behavior patterns and temperament traits. So it was not surprising that ten weeks after his surgery he "felt like" skiing. Spring vacation gave the children a free week, so we headed for one of our favorite ski areas, Vail.

"Surely *you* won't be skiing, Jim, so soon after your surgery?" I asked before leaving.

"The doctor said I could do anything I feel like doing, and I feel well enough to ski," was his confident answer.

"Don't you think you ought to check with him first," I cautiously suggested. "Maybe he didn't mean anything as strenuous as skiing."

"No need to bother him" he assured me. "I'll be careful and not overtax myself. Now don't worry—it'll be good for me."

Chiding myself for being over-protective, I went along and didn't worry. Not until Friday, that is, when a distressed voice from the ski patrol team at the top of the mountain called to tell me they were bringing Jim down in a litter and to meet them at the bottom of Vail Mountain.

"What's the matter, mom?" inquired Jimmy, who had stayed behind with me for the day.

"Oh, nothing, Jimmy. I'm just so tired of your father scaring me," was my reply. "Come on, let's go see what's the matter."

It was a beautiful, clear, sunny day—perfect for skiing. The light, feathery snow crunched underfoot as I nervously paced back and forth in the area to which I expected the ski patrol to descend. When at last they appeared and I looked down at Jim strapped to the specially constructed toboggan-like litter, I knew by his colorless, drawn expression that something serious was wrong. As they unstrapped him and helped him to his feet, he reeled and staggered.

"Mary," he gasped as he collapsed into the car, "I just need to rest. Take me to our room and let me lie down. I'll be all right after I rest."

Without a word, I drove him straight to the emergency room of the tiny Vail hospital, raced in for an oxygen tank, and instructed the nurse on duty to send out a stretcher immediately.

While waiting for the doctor to come out, Jan excitedly explained what had happened on top of the mountain. "Mom, I was scared. Oh, I was so scared. Joy and Jill raced off by themselves to ski that back bowl, and I wanted to go with them, but I knew somebody had to stay with dad. He was so slow. I had to keep looking back to be sure he was still coming. Sometimes he'd stop, and I'd go back to see if he was all right. He was so out-of-breath and tired that we had to stop several times. I finally got him over to the chair-lift so we could ride to a ski patrol station, and dad could hardly breathe by the time we got there. They gave him oxygen. Then we called you and started down the mountain. I didn't know if we'd ever get him down, mom."

I started to comment, but just then I saw the doctor walking through the emergency room door. "Mrs. Irwin, your husband is having a heart attack. We won't know the severity of it for a few days. We'll keep him here until his condition stabilizes; then we'll transfer him to Fitzsimons so his own heart specialist can be with him."

I was not at all surprised. In fact, I had already decided Jim was having another heart attack even though we had been encouraged to believe that his heart surgery would eliminate the possibility for several years. What *did* surprise me was my composure and inner calm throughout the whole ordeal. I was not oblivious to the seriousness of his condition. A second heart attack only ten weeks after the most delicate surgery available in our present culture? Who could be oblivious to the almost obvious implications?

174

Three days later when I heard the army helicopter overhead, I hurried outside. As I watched the helicopter search for a landing spot, I began to cry a little. Even through my tears, however, I thanked God for His goodness. I remembered again that *all things* still work together for good.

The sun was shining brightly as we lifted off the ground. I looked over at Jim. Lidocaine and dextrose were pouring intravenously, while a tube attached to the oxygen bottle ran into his nostrils. Dr. Harry Thomas, cardiologist from Fitzsimons Hospital, sat beside Jim helping him monitored constantly. Glancing out the window again, I could see an impenetrably thick bank of clouds moving in rapidly. A snowstorm was predicted for that evening.

Many times in years gone by my future had looked dark and foreboding, like the distant horizon, but never had it appeared more uncertain than at this moment. As I watched the gathering storm, I remembered those words that had sustained me in many other crises—"Yea, though I walk through the valley of the shadow of death, I will fear no evil."

And I was not afraid.

# Where Credit Is Due

Our husbands, Jim Irwin and Harlan Harris, deserve our sincere appreciation for their patient endurance during nearly two years of preoccupation with the writing of this story. Without their enthusiastic support we could not have undertaken and completed the project.

To our two daughters, Joy, for helpful collaboration on chapter 16, and Lenee Lee, for the tedious typing and retyping of the manuscript, we are deeply grateful.

Betty Skinner was never too busy to pore over both rough and polished copy and offer wise counsel and needed encouragement.

Hope MacDonald and Barbara Logan played important parts in listening to difficult passages and giving constructive suggestions.

Those who faithfully prayed throughout the writing of the story strengthened us more than they knew. Among their number were Muriel Wienbarg, Shirley Henderson, Helene Essendrop, David Harris, Bill and Martha Starkey, Jo Willes, Betty and Phil Wolf, Rhonda Harris, and the ladies of the Ruth Bible Class.

To all those who shed light on forgotten incidents and shared memorable impressions of past years, particularly DiAnne McDaniel and Virginia Palermo, we offer our sincere thanks.

Finally, our lasting gratitude goes to Judy Markham for her remarkable editing skill and Bob DeVries, whose title should read, "encourager of the literary saints."

MARY IRWIN AND MADALENE HARRIS